Single-Sex Schools

Single-Sex Schools

A Place to Learn

Cornelius Riordan

ROWMAN & LITTLEFIELD
Lanham • Boulder • New York • London

Published by Rowman & Littlefield
A wholly owned subsidiary of The Rowman & Littlefield Publishing Group, Inc.
4501 Forbes Boulevard, Suite 200, Lanham, Maryland 20706
www.rowman.com

Unit A, Whitacre Mews, 26-34 Stannary Street, London SE11 4AB

British Library Cataloguing in Publication Information Available

Library of Congress Cataloging-in-Publication Data Available

ISBN 978-1-4758-1363-0 (hardcover)
ISBN 978-1-4758-1364-7 (paperback)
ISBN 978-1-4758-1365-4 (e-book)

♾™ The paper used in this publication meets the minimum requirements of American National Standard for Information Sciences—Permanence of Paper for Printed Library Materials, ANSI/NISO Z39.48-1992.

Contents

Acknowledgments

I am always grateful to the Sociology Department at Johns Hopkins University during the period 1979 to 1981, when I was a postdoctoral fellow. From that time to the present, I have maintained personal relationships with most people who were there at that time. This experience allowed me to look over the edge and understand the potential and the limits of a quantitative sociology.

I want to thank Aaron Pallas who was among the group that I note above, but who has critically read this book and much of my earlier writing. Aaron is a careful, trusted friend, and a tough critic who offered many suggestions to improve this book. I am grateful to George Farkus who I came to know while he was at Penn State, also reviewed an earlier draft of the book and provided many important ideas.

I am always thankful to my wife Arline for providing me continuous love and her own reviews of my thoughts over the past 50 years on a daily basis. Arline and I met at Clark University in the spring of 1965 and we have always cherished and practiced the intellectual tradition that we discovered there together.

Kathleen Ponze and Lauren Hare at the Young Women's Leadership Network provided valuable assistance in obtaining some of the photographs that appear on the cover of the book. The Young Women's Leadership Schools, now numbering 17 across the country, were the first new public single-sex schools to be established beginning in 1996 and have set the standard for scaling up public single sex schools. Ann Rubenstein Tisch is the founder of the YWLN. I am also grateful to Daniel Goodrich who actually took these fine photos of girls in the Young Women's Leadership School in New York.

I am very grateful to the entire staff of Rowman & Littlefield beginning with Tom Koerner, who was willing to publish a short book which is exactly what I wanted to write. Carlie Wall and Staci Zacharski provided excellent support and assistance throughout the production process.

Finally, I want to thank all the advocates and opponents of single-sex schools that I have met over the years since 1985 when I began to research and speak on this topic. The advocates often wanted me to go further in endorsing the value of single-sex schools, and the opponents, of course, wanted to persuade me otherwise. But what is important is that both groups always treated me cordially and respectfully, and I want to thank both sides for their patience and understanding. Like so many things, the solution may lie somewhere between the extremes.

Cummaquid, MA
April 6, 2015

1

✛

Educational Politics and Educational Policy

Most people take coeducation for granted. Typically, their own schooling has been coeducational; often, they have little awareness of single-sex schools. Our political culture reinforces the taken-for-granted character of coeducation. It implies that schools reflecting the variety of society exemplify what is best about democratic societies. Many people also take for granted that coeducation provides equality of educational opportunity for women. Thus, many people regard coeducation as a major milestone in the pursuit of gender equality. Single-sex education, by contrast, appears regressive.

But, in the United States and elsewhere, coeducation began not because of any firm belief in its sound educational effect, but rather because of financial constraints (Tyack and Hansot, 1990; Riordan, 1990). Historically, mixed-sex schools were economically more efficient. In the United States, boys and girls have usually attended the same public schools. This practice originated with the "common" school. Of course, at one time in most countries, only boys received an education. At other times the only education for either boys or girls was single-sex schooling, either public or private.

The social organization of schools is different in each country and different within a country at various historical points. Single-sex schools were common in Europe and elsewhere until the turn of the twentieth century. In the former Soviet Union, coeducation was required after the revolution of 1917, and then single-sex schooling was introduced and required in all urban areas beginning in 1943, and then the country phased back to coeducation in 1954 (Ewing, 2006). In South Korea, a national

1

educational policy was implemented in 1974 requiring that students be randomly assigned to either a single-sex or a coeducational high school (Park et al., 2013).

Once mass and state-supported public education had been established, however, it was clearly the exception for boys and girls to attend single-sex public schools. By the end of the nineteenth century, coeducation was all but universal in U.S. elementary and secondary public schools (see Kolesnick, 1969; Bureau of Education, 1883; Butler, 1910; Riordan, 1990; Tyack and Hansot, 1990). Although single-sex schooling remained as an option in private secondary schools, it had declined with each decade until about 1985, when single-sex schooling was revived in the private sector in the United States and other Western countries. Beginning in 1996, the number of *public* single-sex schools increased from just two to at least one hundred by 2014.

The actual number of these schools is a well-kept secret for several reasons. First, opponents of single-sex schools search painstakingly for this list so that they can attempt to bring the schools to court for violation of the law, and, hence, proponents make little attempt to overpublicize the opening of a single-sex school. Second, the situation is fluid and dynamic, with schools opening or closing each year. Of course, single-sex public schools in the United States are not highly institutionalized, and this makes them more fragile organizational forms than traditional coed schools. However, the Feminist Majority Foundation (Klein et al., 2014) has recently published a complete list of 106 single-sex schools operating between 2011 and 2012. This is easily accessible at http://feminist.org/education/pdfs/IdentifyingSexSegregation12-12-14.pdf.

Wiseman (2008) shows that by 2003, only a few countries across the globe had single-sex schools that made up more than 1 or 2 percent of their total. But there are exceptions where the share of single-sex schools exceeds 10 percent: Belgium, Chile, Singapore, England, Hong Kong, Israel, New Zealand, Australia, Korea, and most Moslem nations. Recently, however, there has been a resurgence of interest in single-sex schools in modern societies across the globe, both in the public and private sector (Riordan, 2002).

Men's and women's colleges also became coeducational largely as a result of economic forces. This continues to be true today as enrollments dwindle in women's colleges. Thus, coeducation has evolved as a commonplace norm, induced not by educational concerns but by other forces. It was within a context of exclusion in the nineteenth century that women's colleges were established. And within this context, the underlying assumption, widely held both then and now, was that women's colleges were a temporary, short-term solution on the road to the eventual achievement of coeducation (see Tidball et al., 1999).

Historically, the gender context of schooling was never subjected to systematic research. The essential force moving society persistently towards coeducation was the belief that coeducation promised greater gender equity and equality of educational opportunity. And, indeed, to the extent that girls and women were excluded entirely from school or where schools for girls were inferior to boys' schools, this movement was essential and beneficial. But, this scenario of female exclusion from schooling no longer holds in Western societies, and this has led to an increase in scientific investigations of the pro and cons of single-sex versus coeducational schooling.

This historical background has provided a protective halo around coeducation as an institution. Currently, this protective halo affects the research strategy and logic for comparing single-sex and mixed-sex schools. The salience of this problem was noted in the report "How Schools Shortchange Women," which was commissioned by the American Association of University Women Educational Foundation (1992; for an update of this study, see AAUW, 1998).

This study examined more than 1,000 publications about girls and education and concluded that bias against females remained widespread in schools into the 1990s, and it was the cause of lasting damage to both educational achievement and self-development. The schools housing this bias were coeducational. Given these findings, one might think that the burden of proof would shift to coeducational schools to first demonstrate that they are free of gender bias, and second, that they are at least as effective as single-sex schools in terms of achievement and gender equity. This would replace the current practice, which requires single-sex schools to show greater effectiveness.

Thus, coeducation as a form of school organization was institutionalized with little regard for educational research or educational theory. Throughout the latter half of the twentieth century, coeducational schools were viewed as politically correct at all levels, especially in the public sector. "Politically correct" is a multifaceted term that often implies the avoidance of forms of expression or action that are perceived to exclude or marginalize groups of people who are socially disadvantaged or discriminated against.

Coeducation is politically correct because it is inclusive of both genders. Single-sex schools are politically incorrect because, by their very nature, boys and girls attend separate schools. But Foucault (1968) cautions, "a political thought can be correct only if it is scientifically painstaking." That is, only if it holds up to objective scientific investigation.

Political correctness can and often does override educational research and sociological theory in the formation of educational policy. Rosemary Salomone (1996) identified this as one of the perils of ideology in her book

Same, Different, Equal: Rethinking Single-Sex Schooling. It is not just about which type of school works best. It is often about what some people think is politically correct. In the long haul, however, educational politics may offer a deceiving foundation for educational policy in the absence of educational research and theory.

Figure 1.1 depicts this relationship among educational politics, research, and policy. As is the case in medical practice, educational practice ideally should be based on sound research and not on educational politics. That is, the arrows of influence from educational politics to educational research and policy should be deleted or at least minimized in a democratic, scientifically oriented society. But this is not the case with regard to the issue of single-sex public education. Educational practice and educational research is dependent on educational politics.[1] I will return to this theme throughout the book.

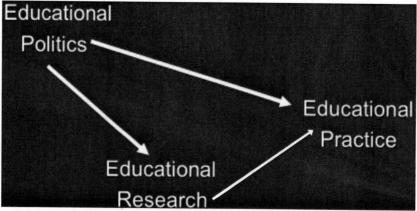

Figure 1.1.   The Role of Educational Politics for Public Single-Sex Schooling

OPPONENTS OF SINGLE SEX SCHOOLS

In the United States, until just recently, it has been virtually impossible to conduct research on *public* single-sex schools because single-sex-school opponents have blocked the opening of such schools that would allow the research to go forward and to address the many questions regarding the relative effectiveness of single-sex and coeducational schooling. Over the past two decades, opponents have continued to point to the lack of evidence favoring single-sex schools, while at the same time actively fighting to undo newly proposed regulations in Title IX as they apply to single-sex schools.

Some critics argue that single-sex schooling smacks of gender segregation and is the same as racial segregation in schools. These two scenarios are not the same. Racial segregation in the public schools in the United States was a willful and intentional and wrongful action made by school boards to legally (de jure) separate schools by race. This was declared unconstitutional by the Supreme Court in the 1954 decision in *Brown v. the Board of Education*. The critics believe that single-sex education should also be unconstitutional in some public sector.

But, students who attend single-sex schools in either the public or the private sector do so by choice. No one is assigning or should be assigning them to these schools (see Salamone, 2003 and 2013 for an excellent discussion of this topic). Indeed, a major problem in most communities in the United States is that students are not given this choice because there are no single-sex schools where they live, and often attempts to open a single-sex school are blocked by opponents who threaten and do take legal action.

The reauthorization of the Elementary and Secondary Education Act (No Child Left Behind) has encouraged and provided funds for a variety of innovative educational programs. Among these programs were single-sex schools and classes. This has required the U.S. Department of Education (USED) to alter the language that guides Title IX in such a way as to remove previously existing legal constraints with regard to public single-sex schools. This new language was released by the USED on October 24, 2006 (http://www.ed.gov/legislation/FedRegister/finrule/2006-4/102506a.html).[2] These new regulations should have provided an expansion of single-sex schools in some public sector and an opportunity to conduct the much needed research.

But, in fact, the expansion of single-sex schools has been effectively blocked by opponents who have challenged the existing research and formed an effective set of alliances and political organizations. Although opposition has always existed since the initial attempt to establish public single-sex academies in Detroit and other cities in the early 1990s, it was largely based on legal objections brought forward by the American Civil Liberties Union (ACLU) and the National Organization of Women (NOW). Drawing upon the Fourteenth Amendment and Title IX, the opponents argued that separate was never equal and always contained a slippery slope. In short, single-sex schools were perceived as a regressive, anachronistic, and deceiving strategy that threatened the hard-earned gains that women had made over the past century. During this decade (1990s), there was very little critique of the research itself.

During the past decade, however, the resurgence of interest in single-sex schools has led to the creation of several stakeholder organizations, some advocate for and others against single-sex schooling. The National

Association of Single Sex Public Education (NASSPE) was founded in 2002, dedicated to the advancement of single-sex public education for both girls and boys. NASSPE was founded by Leonard Sax, and it bears a brain science orientation in all of its activities. In 2007, the European Association of Single-Sex Education (EASSE) was created also to promote single-sex schooling and has held an international conference every other year.

In reaction to these organizations and to the renewed interest in single-sex schooling, a group of U.S. scholars formed the American Council for CoEducational Schooling (ACCES) with a mission of advocating against single-sex schooling and in favor of coeducational schooling. All of these organizations provide news and information on their respective websites, generally supporting their respective goals. EASSE, in particular, has had an effect of increasing the number of single-sex schools all over the world. Any publication by a member of each respective organization finds almost without exception positive results for single-sex schools (NASSPE) or negative results (ACCES).

The implications of this are that we can predict the results of the study by the politics and ideology of the researchers. Neumann (2006) argues that emotion and passion are always a part of empirical research, and that we would be served better if researchers made known their passions and ideological commitments. I would add also they should make known their organizational commitments, especially when these involve leadership and stakeholder positions. Neumann, and more recently Heyneman (2014), demonstrates how this process applies equally to researchers who conduct quantitative or qualitative work.

Heyneman cites the fact that virtually every quantitative study conducted by highly respected pro-school-choice proponents turns out to support (what a surprise) the favorable effects of school choice. Likewise, the research of highly respected researchers opposed to school choice turns out to discover either unfavorable or negligible effects of school choice. And this is exactly how it turns out on the single-sex school issue.

Let me here acknowledge that I have no functional ties to any single-sex schooling organization. Whatever bias I bring to this book is based on thirty years of research, in which my own studies show small but consistently favorable results attained by single-sex schools. Most recently, I served as project director for a study of existing public single-sex schools in the United States. I have studied the effects of single-sex schooling at every level, from kindergarten through college.

This book is not about single-sex classrooms in coeducational schools. Single-sex classrooms were never part of the historical development of single-sex schools and have only come into focus as a result of misguided advocacy by those who argue the case for "hard-wired" brain differences between males and females (Sax, 2005; Gurian and Ballew, 2003). As Salomone (2013) has argued succinctly, these folks "hijacked" the single-sex-school movement right at the point when it was about to become a viable and valuable alternative to regular public coeducational schools.

I am not going to debate the pros and cons of this hard-wired approach in this book because it simply lacks scientific credulity as applied to students in schools.[3] For an excellent discussion of the pitfalls of this approach, see Salamone's excellent article "Rights and Wrongs in the Debate over Single-Sex Schooling" (2013). This aberrant strain towards single-sex classrooms and away from single-sex schools and the application of a hard-wired gender-differentiation approach has brought forth a strong reaction on the part of staunch opponents of single-sex schools. The result is that currently only the most extreme views on single-sex schools (pro and con) have become the focus of the debate.

WHAT IS THIS BOOK ABOUT?

At first glance, whether to expand single-sex schooling might appear to be an obscure issue on the sidelines of the educational policy debates of our times. But it is far from this. In fact, a sizable number of people and political organizations would like to make these schools obscure, but somehow they are "scaling up" rather than down. In 1996, there were only two public single-sex schools left in the United States, and these were both 150 years old. Then, after some early mishaps, these schools began to flourish, and by 2014 there were at least 100 public single-sex schools.

These public single-sex schools are primarily serving poor, urban, black, and at-risk children. About 40 percent are charter schools, but the remainder are regular public schools. The classic and best-known of these is the Young Women's Leadership School in New York City. For boys, the Urban Prep Academies in Chicago and the Eagle Academies in New York City are the best known. The opposition includes the ACLU, NOW, AAUW, ACCES, and the Feminist Majority Foundation.

But, my book is not primarily about this growth. The book takes up the challenge of studying the effectiveness of single-sex schools. First, the real purpose is to free the discussion of its ideological and political baggage and to try to bring some degree of theoretical and empirical balance to the debate. Second, the book attempts to free the debate from advocates of single-sex classrooms and a "brain science" approach and the opponents of this extremist view and focus back on single-sex schools only. Third, the book provides a sociological, theoretical foundation for considering single-sex schools.

This book provides a sociological treatment of the issue. The fundamental argument is that it is the larger school context of all-girls or all-boys that makes the difference. Note that I reject the notion, commonly put forward by other single-sex school advocates, that single-sex classrooms in otherwise coed schools are an effective strategy. This single-sex classroom strategy is based upon a faulty premise that there are physiologically hard-wired gender differences that cause males and females to learn differently.

Moreover, I argue strongly that the notion of single-sex classrooms must always be distinguished as an entirely different and ineffective educational approach compared with single-sex schools. This distinction is critical because both advocates and opponents of single-sex schools, and the media, fail to address this important distinction. A recent article (Pahlke et al., 2014) provides a meta-analysis of single-sex "education" (their term to include both schools and just classrooms). The authors do recognize that these are not the same, but they treat the difference as a difference of "dosage" (their term). In their framework, students in single-sex classrooms in coeducational schools have a smaller dosage of a same-sex environment than students in a single-sex schools. You cannot get a dosage of a single-sex school in a coeducational school.

WHY WRITE THIS BOOK?

One afternoon, I took a taxi from some law offices in downtown Chicago to the airport. In preparation for opening the first public girls' school in Chicago, a law firm had been retained, and they brought me out for the day to work over the topic just in case the school had to go to court. At that time, the opening of a single-sex school was (and still is) a ripe occasion for opponents of single-sex schools to challenge the legal right of the school even before it opened. My Polish Catholic cab driver (as he explained to me later) asked what I was doing in Chicago. I demurred a bit because I thought that single-sex schools would not be of interest to him, but I was very wrong.

He persisted (common among Chicago cab drivers), and so I explained that I had spent the entire afternoon describing and explaining the favorable evidence on single-sex schools to the group of attorneys. He said, "I bet they paid you to tell them what was obvious and why I work night and day." And then he went on to tell me that his sister was depending in part on him to help her pay the tuition to keep her daughter and son in single-sex Catholic schools in Chicago. To him, the value, the explanations, and the evidence were obvious, and he was happy that he was a part of providing his niece and nephew a good education.

So this book is not designed to persuade poor and desperate parents, uncles, and aunts that single-sex schools really do offer an important opportunity. It really is rather obvious to them. But, the book is written in plain, easy-to-understand language, and my hope is that the book will provide social science support for single-sex schools that everybody can understand. I address the book to an audience of open-minded people who haven't had access to a balanced overview of the evidence.

Thus, the purpose is to demonstrate the potential effectiveness of public single-sex schools. In doing this, I do not mean to overlook the important contributions of private single-sex schools and colleges. Private single-sex schools have a rich and long history, and, in fact, most of the research on the topic has been done with private schools. But this research can be applied to the potential of public single-sex schools, as I discuss in Chapter 4. These private schools are well organized and led by the National Coalition for Girls' Schools (http://www.ncgs.org) and the International Boys' Schools Coalition (http://www.theibsc.org). But there is no opposition to these single-sex schools, because they are private.

I argue here that the students who profit most from single-sex schools are disadvantaged, at-risk, urban students, who are largely African American and Latino American. These students and their parents cannot afford private schools. But the schools that do exist, such as Eagle Academy and Urban Prep, have consistently demonstrated outstanding success, as judged by test scores and by the number of student attending and graduating from excellent colleges every year. And yet the opponents claim that the evidence does not support greater effectiveness. I recognize, of course, that the challenge is distinguishing the effects of single-sex schooling from the effects of other factors that may be confounded with it, such as in the case of a charter school that is buffered from bureaucratic red tape and unionized teachers, of an extended school day, or of an extended school year, and so on. I take up these issues in later chapters

Some of the public single-sex schools are members of the private school organizations named above, but most cannot afford the membership fees and the registration and travel to annual meetings. But the problem is not the lack of membership in these supportive private single-sex organizations, but rather it is the strong-armed adamant opposition that I note above.

There was a time in my early experience with single-sex schools that I doubted the value of the results showing favorable outcomes. Like the opponents, initially I did not begin with a favorable image and thought that my own research might be anomalous. I had never attended or even been inside a single-sex school. In my early papers (Riordan, 1984 and 1985), the presentation was muted and downplayed the potential importance of the findings. Sally Kilgore, a noted sociologist of education, was at the presentation of one of these papers at the 1984 meeting of the American Educational Research Association. Her main critique of my paper was really an admonition: she advised me to stop apologizing for the favorable single-sex findings. This was a turning point.

From that point forward, I became a strong advocate for single-sex schools, thinking that the persistent and consistent favorable social science findings favoring single-sex schools would surely have an impact on the educational landscape. Also, I naively thought that these findings would eventually be accepted for what they are by opponents. But, there came a time, as we turned into the twenty-first century, when I realized that data alone would not save single-sex schools.

I came to realize in the fullest probative sense that the folks who oppose single-sex schools will oppose them even if the research showed larger and more impressive results than have actually been found. Even if students in single-sex schools displayed higher test scores in all subject areas than their counterparts attending coeducational schools, even if there was less bullying, less sex-role stereotyping, stronger socioemotional development, greater maturity, greater happiness, and greater occupational success, the opponents would continue to argue the case for coeducational schooling. Educational politics will hold at least equal sway with educational research, as shown above in Figure 1.1.

The implication of this is that we need to at least try to agree on what the research actually shows. Data alone will not be enough when the ultimate decisions on this are made, but they will play an important role. As I will show in the chapters that follow, the data actually do tend to support all of the above hypothetical findings—the effects are small, not large, but they are persistent and consistent. What this means is that the final arbitrator in the single-sex school debate in the public sector will be the U.S. Supreme Court, and I predict that perhaps this issue will arrive there in four or five years.

NOTES

1. This formulation refers to actual practice in and beyond the schools. It is not without flaws. For example, consider the question of what is to be taught as a feature of educational practice. In a democracy, what is to be taught cannot be derived from research; it is inherently a function of politics and values.

2. In December 2014, USED issued a "significant guidance document" addressing questions regarding the 2006 set of new regulations as they apply to single-sex classes (www2.ed.gov/about/offices/list/ocr/docs/faqs-title-ix-single-sex-201412.pdf). Here they cautioned against the use of single-sex classrooms in coeducational schools, providing a set of strict guidelines to school officials who were operating single-sex classrooms.

3. There may be other very effective applications of brain science in medicine, namely, the diagnoses and treatment of human learning or human aging disorders, such as Alzheimer's disease and autism spectrum disorders.

2

✛

Some Simple Assumptions

BASIC DEFINITIONS

Single-sex schools refer to education at the elementary, secondary, or post-secondary level in which males or females attend school exclusively with members of their own sex. Alternatively, males and females may attend all classes separately, even though they may be housed in the same facilities, a phenomenon referred to as a dual academy. An entirely different phenomenon is single-sex classes, whereby schools that are otherwise coeducational provide separate classes for males and females in selected subjects. My argument for single-sex schools is limited entirely to stand-alone schools. *There is no systematic and trustworthy evidence pro or con with regard to single-sex classrooms in coeducational schools.*

Generally, none of these classroom studies reach the level of science that is commonly accepted. All studies of single-sex classrooms lack external validity (generalization) since they are conducted in a specific school with a customized set of single-sex classrooms (such as single-sex classrooms twice a week or three times a week or more, or in reading or math or in both, and with a specific degree of community support or lack of support). There are many permutations of the single-sex classroom idea. Some studies do have internal validity with compelling findings, but there is a great deal of inconsistency.

Moreover, single-sex classrooms do not meet the criteria that I set of establishing an academic culture for the school as a whole. Below, I will argue that it is this academic culture and not gender-differentiated instruction that is the most important factor explaining why students in

12

single-sex schools outperform students in coeducational schools, on average. Single-sex classrooms do not change the culture of the school. It is important to note that private schools have never employed single-sex classrooms in coeducational schools. Single-sex classes emerged in the public sector only, partly because of opposition that made it more difficult to establish a fully functioning single-sex school, and partly because the brain science approach assumes that differentiated instruction for males and females in classrooms is more important (Sax, 2005).

According to Feminist Majority Foundation (Klein et al., 2014), there were at least 106 stand-alone public single-sex schools operating in the United States between 2011 and 2012. There were twice as many all-girls' schools (67) as all-boys' schools (39). These schools served an overwhelming majority of African American and Latino American students (typically 80 to 100 percent). It is quite possible that there are other schools that offer single-sex schooling for boys and girls but within the same physical structure (dual academies). Dual academies are not coeducational schools. Most single-sex public schools serve high percentages of at-risk urban students. And all but two of these schools have opened after 1996. Nearly two-thirds of the nation's public single-sex schools have opened in the last ten years. Some of these schools are charter schools.

ASSUMPTIONS

I begin with several simple but often overlooked assumptions. My point of departure is to reject the notion that certain *inputs* provide equality of educational opportunity or even rise to the claim that they are more effective than other inputs on a prima facie basis. Since Coleman (1968) set forth the need to judge effectiveness and equality claims on the basis of the outcomes rather than inputs, this has become the prevailing and acceptable strategy in educational research (see Fig. 2.1). This strategy, widely accepted in the research community is not always accepted in practice, in policy, or in the law.

Thus, coeducational schools can only be accepted as more effective than single-sex schools if sound, high-quality empirical research can demonstrate this to be reasonably true. The same demand must apply equally to single-sex schools. One must not and should not claim superiority of one or the other on ideological or political grounds. In the end, we judge school effectiveness by looking at outcomes, but school inputs do make the outcomes possible. The gender composition of a school (single-sex or coed) is an input, just like the socioeconomic composition of a school is an input.

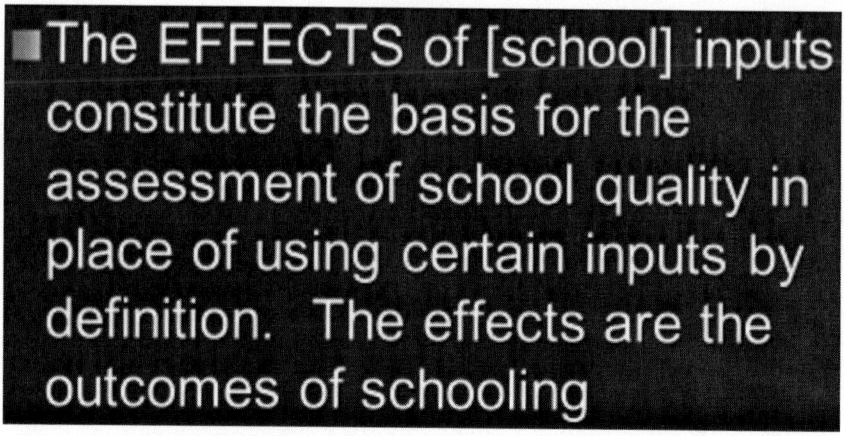

> ■The EFFECTS of [school] inputs constitute the basis for the assessment of school quality in place of using certain inputs by definition. The effects are the outcomes of schooling

Figure 2.1. Defining School Quality: Outcomes

Next, I want to emphasize that single-sex schools are simply one of many options for increasing the effectiveness of schools. For reasons that I will develop throughout the book, single-sex schools will not solve all the problems of developing an effective school, in and of themselves, nor should they be expected to do so. But this is also true of any other reform effort, such as those shown in Figure 2.2. In the United States and elsewhere across the globe, all of the following reforms are employed as strategies for increasing student achievement and socioemotional development: reducing class size, reducing school size, lengthening the school day and/or the school year, providing universal preschool, providing full-day kindergarten, increasing parent involvement, upgrading teacher training and teacher quality, providing greater choice in the form of schools, and offering single-sex schools (see Fig. 2.2). Each of these structural and pedagogical reforms has the potential to contribute in some small way to increasing student achievement and increasing equality of educational outcomes.

Placing single-sex schools in the context of other alternative types of school reform is important for two reasons. First, single-sex schools are often not accepted as a legitimate reform, as noted in the introduction, because of educational politics. But they are, in fact, fully legitimate until the courts rule otherwise. Second, when we look at the empirical outcomes (the effects of single-sex schools), we need to compare these effects to the comparable effects of the other school reforms. Third, the research suggests that no single school reform can, by itself, produce a large effect on student achievement. Single-sex schools should be combined with other structural reforms. This is also true for all the above-mentioned reforms.

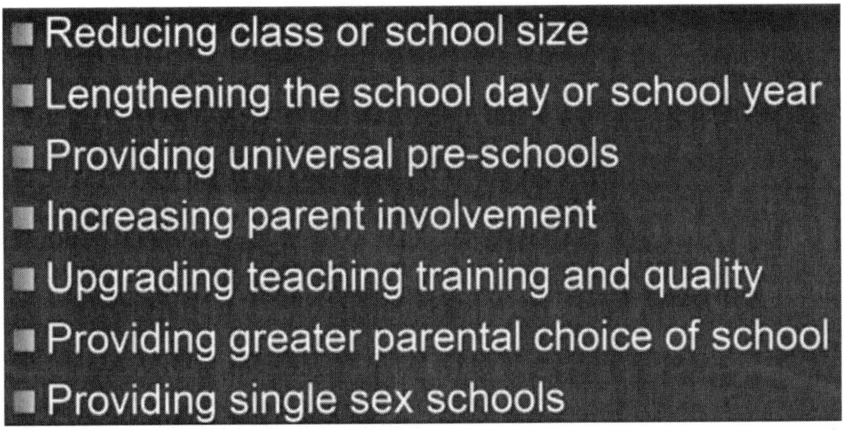

- Reducing class or school size
- Lengthening the school day or school year
- Providing universal pre-schools
- Increasing parent involvement
- Upgrading teaching training and quality
- Providing greater parental choice of school
- Providing single sex schools

Figure 2.2. Defining School Quality: Outcomes

CATHOLIC SCHOOL STUDIES CAN BE EMPLOYED IN THE DEBATE (GENERALLY)

Yet another criticism that opponents have made of single-sex school research is that many studies have been conducted using Catholic schools and very few have been completed using public schools. As noted in Chapter 1, opponents have steadfastly blocked the expansion of public single-sex schools, making it difficult to study them. Consequently, at least in the United States, Catholic schools have been the subject of much single-sex-school research. Although Catholic schools in suburban areas serve predominantly middle- and upper-middle-class students, at least 50 percent of students in Catholic schools since 1980 have been urban, at-risk students and primarily African American or Latino American (O'Keefe and Murphy, 2000; Riordan 2000).

Moreover, all studies referred to in this book are easily able to control for the social class of students and the urbanicity of the school. Inner-city Catholic schools attended mostly by African American and Latino American students are similar to inner-city public schools, and comparisons of students in these inner-city Catholic schools who attend either single-sex or coeducational schools provide strong evidence of what the results would be in public schools. I make this point here because several of these studies that I will cite in this chapter were conducted on inner-city Catholic schools, where there are a sufficient number of single-sex schools.

IMPORTANT METHODOLOGICAL ISSUES OF SOCIAL SCIENCE

In science, we must be able to show that an independent variable is related to a dependent variable and that the results must not be spurious, which means that the relationship results from other factors other than the independent variable. So, with single-sex schools, we must be able to establish that they are related to higher academic achievement or better socioemotional development and that this is *NOT* due to some other factor.

For example, let's say we find that students in single-sex schools do better than students in a coeducational schools, but this may be simply because the students in the single-sex schools are more affluent, with access to better resources at home and better preparation prior to school, or they may be better motivated, either out of the desperation that often accompanies poverty or the aspiration that often accompanies affluence. The point is that we must control for these other factors. There are only two ways to do this.

The best method is to employ the gold standard of science—*a randomized experiment*. Within a geographic area, such as a city or a country, all students would be randomly assigned to either a single-sex or coeducational school. And teachers also would be randomly assigned. This is how most research is conducted in medical science. So long as the number of units is sufficiently large, random assignment rules out the possibility that students in the single-sex schools will be more affluent or more motivated. Of course, this is not easy to do in the field of education, because most parents, students, and teachers would object. And, indeed, it is not done often, but is has been done in South Korea since 1974, and we will examine the result of this experiment below.

In most cases, however, random assignment is not possible, and a second scientific strategy is employed, namely, *statistical control for other relevant variables*. In this case, we first establish that there is a relationship between the type of school and the outcome, and then we control for as many of the likely other variables as possible. These other variables would include socioeconomic status of the home and of the school, family structure, family functioning, family involvement in the school, previous test scores, and so on. But note that it is not possible to control for every possible variable that might change the relationship between type of school (single-sex or coed) and the outcomes. For example, the age of school entry in months or how often parents read to their children before school began might possibly make a difference in favoring single-sex schools.

Random assignment rules all of these other factors out (which is why it is the gold standard), but statistical control cannot ever fully do this. However, I want to emphasize here that controlling for six to ten of the key other variables is usually adequate to provide reasonable justification that the relationship of school type to the outcomes is not spurious. I shall refer herein to both types of control. *But, I cannot emphasize enough that without one or the other form of control, all conclusions about single-sex schools (or any other independent variable) must be dismissed.*

When we conclude that the relationship between school type and the outcome is not the result of other factors, we usually say that it is statistically significant. Even in a random experiment, there is always some chance of being wrong in drawing this conclusion, so a relationship is only significant if the probability of being wrong is very small (less than 5 times out of 100, or .05). When we cannot establish this, we say that the potential relationship between school type and the outcome is *null*, meaning that there is no relationship. This would imply that students would be equally served by a single-sex or a coeducational school.

Relationships can be statistically significant but so small in magnitude that they are trivial. This happens often if the size of the sample is extremely large. The reverse is also true: a relationship can be very strong as judged by a correlation or regression coefficient, but be insignificant, if the sample is very small. I take this up again in Chapter 3.

SELECTION BIAS

A related issue is that the study of schools must address the dilemma that good students always seem to find good schools and good teachers. I use the word "good" here as a shorthand term to mean "highly effective" and "high quality." Although these attributes are difficult to measure and difficult to conceptualize, we all recognize from our own personal experiences that good teachers and good schools are real. A great deal of everyday conversation among neighbors and friends is an exchange about the quality of teachers and schools.

This raises serious questions in the comparison of school types. This is true regardless of whether we are studying private or public schools. All parents desire the best education for their children that they can manage to obtain given their resources. Affluent parents may choose to send their children to private schools or buy a home in an affluent community known for excellent schools. Or they will make a choice and send their child to a public charter school. In either case, these schools may have better-qualified and better-motivated teachers, a more effectively designed and implemented curriculum, and classmates who also value academics, and even if all this is not true, they will have made a choice and selection of the school that differentiates them from all other students who are simply assigned to a school by the district office. Following Coleman, however, a good school is judged by outcomes, not inputs.

But most of this selection process is highly dependent upon the social class and motivation of parents. This means that even if they cannot afford a private school or a house in the suburbs or are not lucky enough to win a lottery spot in a charter school, they will still be able to provide educational, financial, and psychological support in the home.

And so, when we discover that students who attend a certain type of school have higher test scores, higher graduation rates, higher acceptance rates into colleges, or higher levels of self-esteem, it is difficult to determine if this is the result of good schools or good homes (see Fig. 2.3). This means that we need studies that control for home effects, either through random assignment (as in South Korea) or through statistical control.

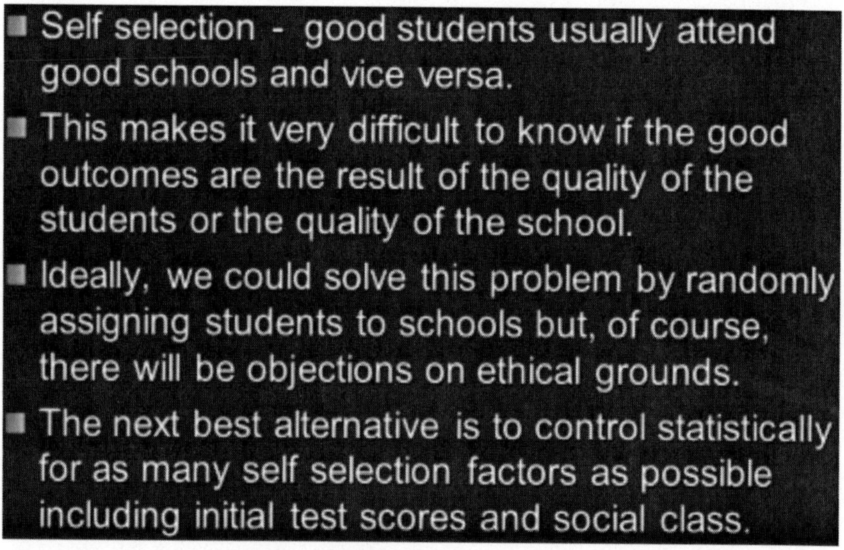

- Self selection - good students usually attend good schools and vice versa.
- This makes it very difficult to know if the good outcomes are the result of the quality of the students or the quality of the school.
- Ideally, we could solve this problem by randomly assigning students to schools but, of course, there will be objections on ethical grounds.
- The next best alternative is to control statistically for as many self selection factors as possible including initial test scores and social class.

Figure 2.3.   Basic Issues of School Effect Studies

3

✛

What Are School Effects and How Do We Measure Them?

Most people think that the quality of a school does make a difference in the academic achievement and well-being of students, and that it is relatively easy to distinguish a good school from a bad one. In practice, this does not turn out to be true. For one thing, as Goodlad (1984: 247) points out, "the didactics of the classroom . . . are . . . very much the same from school to-school." This is true, despite the fact that they are viewed as being very different by principals, teachers, students, and parents.

At the extremes, of course, good schools and bad schools are easy to identify. Everyone knows that an elite independent private school is a good school relative to a typical public school in the inner city. Everyone knows that a public school in which the average per pupil expenditure is $30,000 is a good school relative to a public school in which per pupil expenditure is only $6,000. Kozol (1991) properly calls these kinds of comparisons "savage inequalities." Within these extremes, however, it is much more difficult to discern inequalities and effectiveness between schools.

In this chapter, I focus on "school effects"—specifically, those effects on students that are the result of attending different types of schools. Schools differ in per pupil expenditure, size, governance (public or private), quality of the teachers, the administration, and the students, the type and quality of the curriculum, the quality of the extracurriculum, the length of the school day and the school year, whether they are regular or charter public schools, and whether they are single-sex or coeducational. To a large degree, all of these factors influence the degree to which a school provides a pro-academic culture or an anti-academic culture, or

19

somewhere in between these cultural norms that guide the effectiveness of schools.

Throughout the discussion, an important distinction is made between the magnitude of school effects that exist for disadvantaged as opposed to advantaged students. In due course, we will discover that between-school effects are relatively small, compared to the larger effects of race and socioeconomic status of parents. Sometimes these effects are null (zero). However, school effects are consistently much larger for nonwhites, disadvantaged, and otherwise at-risk students.

THE DIFFERENCE BETWEEN HOME AND SCHOOL EFFECTS

From the earliest days of both public and private schooling, everyone must have been aware that differences between homes affect school performance. Even in the first "public" schools in England (which were what we now call private schools), the home background of students varied among the very wealthy. Certainly, in the history of public schools in the United States and elsewhere, student home background varied greatly and was related to educational outcomes. The home background of a student, especially socioeconomic status, varies greatly and strongly influences success and failure in school. Literature and history provide many descriptive examples of the educational paths of children from rich and poor homes.

By contrast, the idea of "school effects" is a recent construct. For school effects to occur, there must exist "school differences" that are real and recognized. For example, most people have assumed that real differences in material resources have always existed between public and private schools. With regard to public schools, however, at least in the United States, these possible differences were masked by an ideology and a policy of "common schools." Well into the twentieth century, it was thought that students attended schools that were very much the same in terms of resources, teachers, curriculum, and so on. This was prior to the great expansion of schooling and during a time in which most towns and cities had only a single high school.

There were several transformations of the educational landscape that actually created school differences and made possible the notion of a school effect. Perhaps the most important of these forces was the expansion of schooling at the turn of the twentieth century. This process soon led to the need for multiple junior and senior high schools and further to the need for several different types of schools—the classical high school, the vocational high school, and the comprehensive high school. The differential curricula in each of these types of schools were sufficient to produce a school effect.

A related development was the creation of suburban schools. The development of the suburbs is coterminous with the exodus of the middle class from the central cities during the latter half of the twentieth century. This process has been characterized as "white flight," mainly from the laws requiring school desegregation and forced busing. In any event, suburban schools were initially white and middle class, with relatively higher property and income wealth than city schools.

Consequently, suburban schools often were provided with better resources than city schools. They were also newer, they had better facilities, and they were usually able to pay higher salaries to teachers. Over the past several decades, the suburbs have become increasingly diverse as nonwhites also have moved out of the inner city. Many inner suburban areas are predominantly African American or Latino because many black middle-class families, and black working-class families with stable employment histories, took advantage of better jobs and lessened housing discrimination to leave the inner city in large numbers (Wilson, 1987).

Although much work on school effects compares public schools of varying wealth measured by per pupil expenditure, there are many other ways to think about school effects. Among other possibilities would be comparison of public and private schools, small and large schools, charter and regular public schools, and single-sex and coeducational schools. Each of these has received considerable attention in the study of school effects.

HOW DO WE MEASURE A SCHOOL EFFECT?

A school effect is the difference between what the average student would gain (or lose) by attending a single-sex school in comparison to a comparable coeducational school, assuming that the schools and students were essentially equal in all other important characteristics (determined either through random assignment or statistical control). The gains could refer to academic achievement and/or socioemotional development, or other possible outcomes, such as a reduction of bullying in the school.

It is important to understand that this is entirely different from the effect of sex or socioeconomic status (SES) on achievement. For example, the effect of SES is typically two or three times greater than the effect of a school type. And the effect of school type is usually greater for low-SES students.

This typical pattern is displayed in Figure 3.1, where the effect of SES per se is one year (students from a high-SES home obtain one full year more education than students in a low-SES home), but the effect of school type per se is zero for high-SES students and one-half year of greater educational attainment for low-SES students. Students with average (M for middle) SES would gain a relatively small amount of one-quarter of a year more education in single-sex schools. Although the estimates in Figure 3.1 are fictional, for simplicity, they are, in fact, very close to the average actual results as discussed in Chapters 4 and 5.

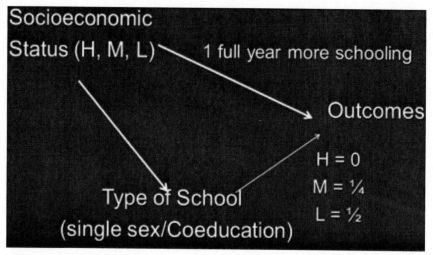

Figure 3.1.   School Type to Outcomes, Controlling for Socioeconomic Status (H, M, L)

Note that we assume the schools would be equal in terms of financial and instructional resources, and that the students would be equal in terms of motivation, aptitude, and past achievement, and student home background would be equal in terms of SES, family structure and functioning, parental involvement, and many other factors associated with home life. This would require either a randomized field experiment or strong statistical adjustments. In fact, this presents an enormous hurdle, and possibly even an insurmountable challenge, but it is the only way to determine the existence and the size of a single-sex school effect.

This implies that we need to think more carefully about what we might expect to find in terms of a single-sex school effect. *Fifty years of sociological research on this topic of school effects has consistently determined that school effects are relatively small* (Riordan, 2004; Borman and Dowling, 2010).[1] By this we mean the factors that influence student achievement and socioemotional development may have less to do with differences among schools and more to do with differences between homes and students themselves, and within schools. This does not mean that the differences between schools are not important but simply that the magnitude of these between-school effects are smaller than differences between homes and within schools (Riordan, 2004).

Generally, the average effect of the home background (including SES, race, and other family characteristics) on both the academic and socio-emotional development of students is three times as great as the effect that might be attributed to differences between schools. That is, differences between single-sex schools and coeducational schools, or Catholic and public schools, or large and small schools, or any other school-to-school comparison is likely to be small compared to differences between homes (see Riordan, 2004).

In addition, the average effect of what we refer to as the "within-school" difference is also three times as great as the difference between the two types of schools, on average. Within-school differences refer to factors that vary within each school, such as teacher quality and ability group placement. And, of course, there are also major differences between the students themselves in terms of IQ, motivation, aspirations, and bio-physiological factors, such as motor skills. And there are also important differences and effects of peer group membership. But, here I only want to convey that a school effect is relatively small when considered by itself.

Part of the problem is conceptual and part of it is statistical. Conceptually, it would be naive to think that *all* students will benefit from single-sex schooling at any grade level. Some students will do quite well in single-sex schools compared to coeducational schools, but others may react negatively or poorly, and for some, it will make no difference. And some of this single-sex school effect will be conditioned by student characteristics and the unique characteristics of each school. For example, boys might do much better than girls in single-sex schools, or vice versa.

And when you average these positive and negative effects for all the students, it should not be surprising that the effect is often small. But note, if the effect is statistically positive in favor of single-sex schools, it strongly suggests that most student do very well, and only some students do poorly, and for a few students it makes no difference. *Or, even more likely, as I will demonstrate in Chapter 5, at-risk students may do very well in single-sex schools, but others gain nothing, or make only small gains. This too would average out to small gains overall.*

Part of this small-school effect is also statistical. When you look at the effect of single-sex and coeducational schools, the variable is a dichotomy (it only has two values), and hence there is very little mathematical variation in the variable. Statistically, the standard deviation of a dichotomous variable is quite small (between zero and one), and this in turn affects the computations of the standard errors, and thus the statistical significance—this is why we often obtain null studies in looking at school effects (Allison, 1999).

We cannot change the school-type variable (it will always only have two values), but we can and must recognize this limitation for interpreting the results. Specifically, if we found that there were an equal number of high-quality studies favoring either single-sex or coeducational schools or that the results were null (one-third for each), then it would be reasonable to conclude that there is not relationship between the school type and the outcomes.

However, if we find that the majority of studies either favor single-sex schools or they are null (very few or none favoring coeducational schools), and bearing in mind that statistical significance is constrained by the dichotomous nature of the school type variable, then we should conclude (I believe) that the null studies are more likely to favor single-sex schools. This is exactly what we shall see in the pages ahead.

And, there is an additional reason for obtaining small school effects. Most of the best research on school effects is limited to one or two years of students attending a single-sex or coeducational school. This is true for the study of any type of school effect. Part of the reason for this is the cost of doing high-level research of this type each year. But, the cost is made even more complicated because students change schools often and thus are lost to the study from year to year. And finally, whether they change schools or not, student data (especially test score data) are lost with each year as a result of absences from school or refusals to continue participation in the study (often on the part of parents). For this reason, these small school effects do need to be estimated for a longer period of time in order to evaluate their true potential impact.

If we are able to demonstrate that there is a consistent and valid single-sex school effect that is small and occurs each year vis-à-vis attending a coeducational school, the four-year effect will probably be four times, whatever the small single-year effect is. In other words, if the one-year single-sex school effect is one-quarter of a grade equivalent, an average student might gain as much as one full year worth of education by attending a single-sex school rather than attending a coeducational school. All of this assumes that there is a valid and consistent small single-sex school effect.

Finally, there are two other considerations that have been widely addressed in the school effects literature. First, most of the high-quality studies of single-sex versus coeducational schools have been conducted employing high school students. Learning rates are greatly reduced by the sophomore year of high school and have been shown to be much higher in the elementary grades (Jencks, 1985). Therefore, these small school effects may be misleading as a benchmark for determining when a little is a lot or just a little.

Finally, there is a controversy over what constitutes an effect size of substantive importance. An effect size (ES) is a general term for various statistics that estimate the magnitude of the relationship between an independent variable and the dependent variable. A percentage difference is perhaps the simplest way to express this estimate of an effect. A correlation is another way to express an ES. Note that just as a percentage difference ranges from 0 to 100, a correlation ranges from 0 to plus or minus 1.0.

Typically, the difference between two groups on some dependent variable, such as a test score, is converted into an ES by dividing the test score difference in raw units by the pooled standard deviation. This transforms the difference into a metric that ranges between 0 and plus or minus 1.0. An ES can be higher than 1.0, but not often. Typically, an ES between .10 and .20 is considered small, but researchers differ over whether this is substantively important or not.

Sound educational research has shown that a standard ES of .10 on gains from the end of sophomore year to the end of senior year of high school is equivalent to one full year of learning by the average public school student in the United States (Hoffer et al., 1985).[2] Applying this standard, an ES difference of .10 or greater between students in single-sex and coeducational schools would be substantially important, whether as a gain score or cross-sectional effect, assuming that it was statistically significant. Other researchers (see references in Chapter 4) employ an older rubric set by Cohen (1988) that sets a threshold of .2 for an ES only reaching the status of "small." That is to say, an ES would only be considered small if it reached the .2 level.

Bloom and colleagues (2006) argue that these conventions must be treated with caution. An ES of .10 might be of great importance in some contexts, but not in others. For example, they point to a well-known study of the effect size of using aspirin to reduce the risk of heart attacks, and the ES in favor of using aspirin was only .06. Most physicians and their patients accept this as a substantively important effect. They recommend treating an ES of .15 in educational research as small and substantively important.

I believe that school effects researchers (that is, professionals who specialize in studying the effects of schools) think that Cohen's benchmark may miss important and substantive differences, as I have argued above. Any set of schools that can consistently produce an ES of .15 (estimated as equivalent to a one-year gain in math or verbal knowledge) compared to a set of otherwise comparable schools in terms of social class and initial ability, should command our attention. This is especially true if the students involved are high-risk, disadvantaged youth. In any event, the interpretation of a small ES (.10 to .20) is the crux of the issue.

All of these limitations pertaining to the study of school effects apply equally to any type of school effect. Opponents of single-sex schools often point to the small or null effects that have been reported in the literature. But, they fail to point out that all of the alternatives that they offer, such as small school size and high teacher quality, also have small and many null effects. Thus, the fact that the single-sex school effects are often small is not a basis for dismissing them. Moreover, the small effects favoring single-sex schools that I will provide shortly are quite bountiful compared to small school effects favoring coeducational schools, which are virtually nonexistent (see Fig. 3.2).

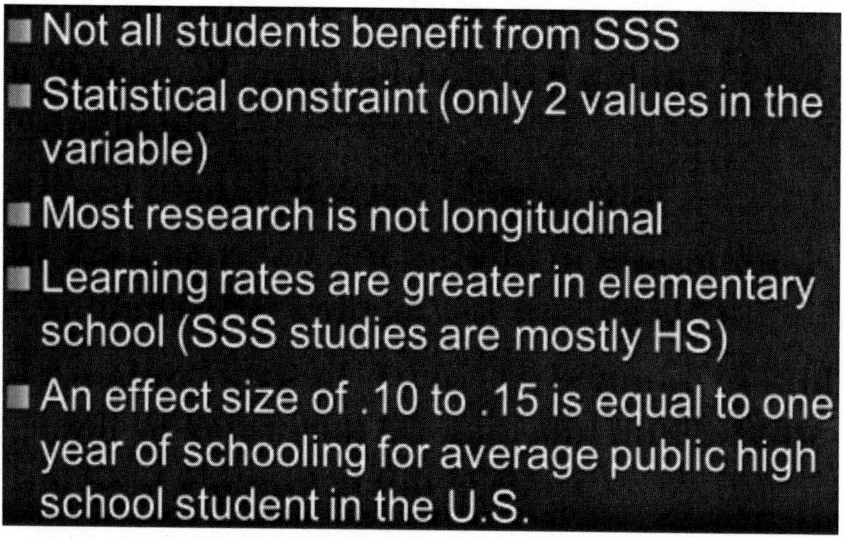

■ Not all students benefit from SSS

■ Statistical constraint (only 2 values in the variable)

■ Most research is not longitudinal

■ Learning rates are greater in elementary school (SSS studies are mostly HS)

■ An effect size of .10 to .15 is equal to one year of schooling for average public high school student in the U.S.

Figure 3.2.   School Effects Are Small. Why?

NOTES

1. Using multilevel methodology, Borman and Dowling (2010) have shown that the school effects in the Coleman report (Coleman et al., 1966) are actually larger than previously reported. However, this study is an exception to the above-stated assertion that between-school effects are generally smaller. Moreover, Coleman and colleagues (1966) actually indicated clearly that between-school effects are much larger than social background among both African American and Latino American students (see Tables 3.221.1 and 3.221.2 in the report, and my discussion in Chapter 5).

2. This equivalent of a .10 ES being equal to about a one-year gain in test scores for the average public school student is estimated by using the High School & Beyond (http://nces.ed.gov/surveys/hsb/) data 1980 to 1982, end of sophomore year to end of senior year. Alexander and Pallas (1985) found a slightly smaller school effect using exactly the same data (ES = .08, translating into about two-thirds of a year of education), which they considered trivial.

4

What Do We Know about Single-Sex School Effects?

On the basis of my own research, and of other studies across the globe, we do have good reason to conclude that single-sex schools help to improve student achievement. Across a wide range of high-quality studies, students in single-sex schools, compared to their counterparts in coeducational schools, have been shown to have higher academic achievement and more favorable socioemotional outcomes (Mael et al., 2005; Riordan 1990, 1994a, 1994b; Salomone, 2003; for opposing conclusions, see Marsh 1989, 1991; Smithers and Robinson, 2006; Halpern et al., 2011; Pahlke et al., 2014).

In their Catholic school study, Lee and Bryk (1986, 1989; Bryk et al., 1993) analyzed data from a large national sample of schools called High School & Beyond (HSB; see note 2 in Chapter 3). These students represented the high school graduating class of 1982. They compared student outcomes in single-sex and coeducational Catholic schools by statistically controlling for social class, race, and other background characteristics. The results are summarized in the Figure 4.1.

The outcomes in this figure contain academic achievement in various subject areas, socioemotional indicators, school behaviors and attitudes, and course enrollments. Effects towards the right of .0 favor single-sex schools, effects to the left favor coeducational schools. You can see immediately that very few effects favor coeducational schools.

This study is included among a high-quality meta-analysis of the forty best background controlled studies by Mael and colleagues (2005) and in the recent meta-analysis by Pahlke and colleagues (2014) that I will review below. But, I prefer to begin by focusing attention on this single study because it is easier to understand and visualize.

Despite being dated and limited to Catholic schools, this figure allows us to summarize the overall results more graphically than I can by presenting the results of a meta-analysis of the forty best studies. The Lee and Bryk study actually shows the overall average results from the past thirty years best, even though it is limited to a single study in 1982. The results shown in Figure 4.1 employed statistical control for more than a dozen background variables.

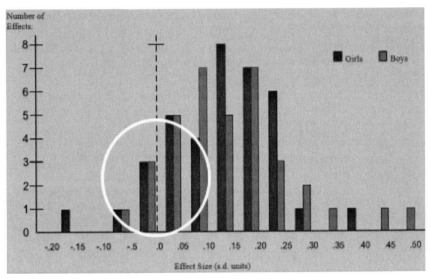

Figure 4.1.   Effect Sizes of Single-Sex Schooling from Lee and Bryk (1986)

Lee and Bryk (1989) found sixty-five of seven-four separate dependent-variable effects to be in favor of single-sex schools. Thirty (30) of seventy-four effects obtained an effect size (ES) of .18 or higher, favoring single-sex schools, equally distributed among boys and girls, and the mean ES was .13, favoring single-sex schools. The distribution of these effects is approximately normal. The results are approximately equal for boys and girls. Many of the effects hover close to zero and are statistically null. Virtually all of the effects favoring coeducational are null.

To give you some idea of the importance of these findings by Lee and Bryk, we know from previous studies of school effects that an ES of .15 is equal to one year of schooling for an average public school student, as noted previously in Chapter 3. In the case of Lee and Bryk, they compared the gains made over a two-year period. Of course, their average effect was .13, so assuming the gains they found held over a four-year period of high school, the effects shown in Figure 4.1 would double, and this would amount to about two years of school difference between those students who attended a single-sex Catholic school and those who attended a co-educational Catholic school.

It is important, however, in keeping with my earlier cautions, to note that the above study by Lee and Bryk did receive a frontal attack by Marsh (1989), who examined the very same data and was able to demonstrate null effects. Marsh added many more control variables and set different criteria for statistical significance than Lee and Bryk did, probably overcontrolling for the background variables. This same type of exchange occurred in a study by Riordan (1985), which showed favorable results for students in Catholic single-sex schools compared to their counterparts in Catholic coeducational schools, with entirely different data from the high school class of 1972 and Marsh (1991), who reanalyzed these data, again adding many more control variables and obtaining null results. All of these studies are part of the systematic meta-analysis that I will report below.

A key control variable employed by Marsh was the educational expectations of the student. Both Lee and Bryk (1986) and Riordan (1985) conceived of educational expectations as an outcome variable. This is a reasonable conceptualization of the process: single-sex schools will affect not only grades, test scores, and emotional growth but also cognitive expectations. The variables were actually measured as outcomes, since students had been in single-sex or coeducational schools for at least two years prior to the actual time of measurement.

On the other hand, Marsh is also correct in conceiving that students who attend single-sex schools may have higher educational expectations to begin with and that is why they choose the school in the first place. This is a common problem in educational research that cannot be ignored, and I wish to bring it to your attention at this point.

Is there a way out of this conundrum? Note that even when Marsh employs educational expectations as a prior control variable the results do not favor coeducational schools, but rather are null. When they are not employed, as in Lee and Bryk (1986) or Riordan (1985), the results show small, favorable single-sex schools effects. These results are due to many factors (not just this dual applicability of educational expectations), but my major point is that even when the research is put to the ultimate test of controlling for a variable that was measured as an outcome, *the results do not favor coeducational schools.*

Recently, however, research in South Korea provides a unique opportunity to examine the effects of single-sex schooling as a randomized experiment. In 1974, the South Korean government passed an equalization policy aimed at reducing high levels of inequality in the country. As it applies to education, the equalization policy of 1974 requires that beyond middle school (grade 8) students are randomly assigned to high schools within their districts. It applies to all schools, public and private, and to coeducational and single-sex schools.

Students cannot choose to attend a single-sex or a private school. If students move, they are again subject to random assignment. Therefore, there are no significant differences between students in any of the schools. The policy is controversial in Korea, and I use this example only to demonstrate the outcomes in a country where a randomized assignment has been used. About 50 percent of the schools in South Korea are single-sex, and South Korea is a top performer in virtually all international comparisons, such as the Program for International Student Assessment (PISA)

Park and colleagues (2013) conducted a study of single-sex and coeducational schools in Korea. They limited their research to Seoul because it contains the largest number of students and schools. The sample contained sixty-eight all-boys' school, sixty all-girls' schools, and sixty-eight coeducational schools. Park and Behrman checked on the integrity of the random assignment across the single-sex and coeducational schools and reported no differences in home background or in the socioeconomic composition of the schools or in prior achievement. They concluded (447):

> The three-level hierarchical model shows that attending all-boys schools or all-girls schools, rather than coeducational schools, is significantly associated with higher average scores on Korean and English test scores. Applying the school district fixed-effects models, we find that single-sex schools produce a higher percentage of graduates who attended four-year colleges and a lower percentage of graduates who attended two-year junior colleges than do coeducational schools. The positive effects of single-sex schools remain substantial, even after we take into account various school-level variables, such as teacher quality, the student-teacher ratio, the proportion of students receiving lunch support, and whether the schools are public or private.

Several other studies on single-sex schools in Korea have been conducted in the past few years.

Kim and Law (2011) employed data from the 2006 PISA. PISA has been conducted every three years since 2000 and examines the cognitive skills of 15-years-old students in about sixty-five countries. In their rigorous multivariable study of Korea and Hong Kong, Lim and Law (2011:99) concluded that "attending a boys' school appears to be beneficial to maths achievement in both Korea and Hong Kong, whereas attending a girls' school is advantageous in this respect only in Korea." Bear in mind, of course that only in Korea are students randomly assigned to schools. Here Lim and Law (like Park et al., 2013) found favorable results for both males and females. However, in yet another study Pahlke and colleagues (2014) found null results using a different but comparable set (TIMMS) in Korea for 2003 and 2007. Thus once again, we get the familiar null or small favorable effects for single-sex schools.

The Organisation for Economic Co-operation and Development (OECD), which manages the collection of PISA data, explored the question of why schools like those in South Korea are successful and then identified four key factors (OECD, 2009). Among the factors they identified were autonomy and discipline. They report that schools with better disciplinary climates tend to achieve higher scores in reading. And they show, not surprisingly, that Korea has the second- highest level of discipline of all countries in the study (Poland is average, and Japan is first).

Below I will identify greater order and discipline as one of the reasons for greater achievement in single-sex schools. Here I use it to complete this discussion, showing that the only country in the world that randomly assigns students to single-sex and coeducational schools had the second-highest levels of discipline and the first- or second-highest levels of achievement in reading, mathematics, and science in 2009 (OECD, 2009).

SYSTEMATIC REVIEWS OF RESEARCH

In anticipation of an increase in the number of public single-sex schools, the U.S. Department of Education (USED) contracted with the RMC Research Corporation to conduct a descriptive study of existing single-sex public schools. One component of this large study conducted for USED in the United States is a systematic review (meta-analysis) of the entire research literature on single-sex schooling at that time. I directed the overall project, but the meta-analysis was conducted by the American Institutes for Research and was completed in 2005.

A meta-analysis is a collection of many studies on a single topic to determine the *average effects* that were found drawing upon all studies. The Lee and Bryk study discussed earlier is a single study that by itself might be an anomaly (exception), and this is why we conduct a meta-analysis. To be included in this quantitative review, a study had to utilize appropriate measurement and statistical methods. Thus, a study had to include statistical controls for individual characteristics (e.g., socioeconomic status, individual ability, and age) and school characteristics that might explain the differences between single-sex and coed schools.

Ultimately, only forty published studies met the inclusion criteria and were thus retained. Reasons for excluding the other studies included (1) failure to operationalize the intervention properly, (2) failure to apply statistical controls during the analyses, (3) work that was qualitative in nature rather than quantitative, (4) work written in a foreign language, (5) failure to draw comparisons between single-sex and coed schools, or (6) students who were not of elementary, middle, or high school age.

The results of the systematic review were organized by six broad topical areas: (1) concurrent academic achievement, (2) long-term academic achievement, (3) concurrent socioemotional development, (4) long-term socioemotional development, (5) perceived school culture, and (6) subjective satisfaction. Most of the outcome measures in the forty studies were in either the concurrent academic accomplishment or the concurrent socioemotional development areas. This book discusses only these two categories because of the small number of outcomes in the other categories. None of the researchers on this study had any ideological or organizational ties to single-sex schools or to the opponents of single-sex schools.

If the findings of a study all supported single-sex schooling for a given outcome variable, it was coded as "pro–single-sex." If a study's findings all supported coeducation for a given outcome variable, it was coded "pro-coeducation." A study was coded "null" if there were no statistically significant differences between the single-sex and coeducation outcomes, and it was coded "mixed" if the study had statistically significant findings in opposite directions for different subgroups. For example, a study was coded mixed if the findings supported single-sex schooling for boys but supported coeducation for girls. Or, if the findings supported single-sex schooling at one grade level but supported coed schooling at another grade level, the study was coded mixed. If a study had findings that were both pro–single-sex and null, it was coded pro–single-sex. If a study had findings that were both pro-coeducation and null, it was coded pro-coeducation. The results are summarized in Figure 4.2.

| | Percentage of Outcomes | | | |
Outcome Measure	Pro-SS	Pro-CE	Null	Mixed
Short Term Academic Accomplishment	35%	2%	53%	10%
Short Term Socio-Emotional Development	45%	10%	39%	6%

Note. SS = single-sex. CE = coed. Source: http://www.ed.gov/rschstat/eval/other/single-sex/index.html

Figure 4.2.   Summary of Systematic Literature Review Findings

You can see that the results of the systematic review mirror the results that I have just shown to you from Lee and Bryk. There are virtually no outcomes favoring coeducational schools; a few mixed results; the remaining outcomes are evenly divided between those favoring single-sex schools or null results. And, of course, we should now bring to bear the point I made earlier as to why some studies obtain null results by controlling for variables, such as educational expectations, that are, in fact, both an outcome and an input to single-sex schools. Bear in mind also, that most of these studies are cross-sectional.

The results clearly do not favor coeducational schools, just as was depicted in the Lee and Bryk study. But, employing the logic that I presented earlier, we must assume that most of the null studies would lean towards single-sex schooling, as shown in the Lee and Bryk study. Contrary to the selective interpretations made by other researchers with reference to this study (Bracey, 2006; Smithers and Robinson, 2006; Signorella et al., 2013), who concluded that the results are equivocal, those who actually did the study concluded that the results of the review demonstrate small to moderately favorable outcomes for single-sex schools vis-à-vis coeducational schools. According to Mael and colleagues (2005:86): "The preponderance of studies in areas such as academic accomplishment (both concurrent and long term) and adaptation or socioemotional development (both concurrent and long term) yields results lending support to SS [single-sex] schooling." In the executive summary (xv) of the report, they write, "this minimal to medium support for SS schooling applies to both males and females and in studies pertaining to both elementary and high schools."

Signorella and colleagues (2013) reported a strong critique of the Mael and colleagues (2005) review. Despite an obvious effort to demonstrate flaws in the entire Mael and colleagues paper (method, inclusion or exclusion of studies, interpretation of studies, and results), Signorella and colleagues essentially reached the same conclusions that I have suggested above and will below. They find null results in mathematics achievement and self-concept, but a controlled ES of .18 for verbal achievement. They explicitly apply the Cohen guideline noted in Chapter 3 to conclude that this is too small to be considered important. There are no results in the critique showing more favorable results for coeducational schools.

A more recent meta-analysis by Pahlke and colleagues (2014: 23) examined 184 studies along 16 different outcomes and concluded that "there is little evidence of an advantage of SS schooling for girls or boys for any of the outcomes." They employ the .2 ES threshold in drawing these conclusions of no advantage for single-sex schooling. Nonetheless, it is a thorough piece of research and contains important findings. The analysis distinguished between controlled and uncontrolled studies, and it correctly emphasized the importance of the controlled studies.

Most of the ESs for the control studies are below .2, and often close to zero, but rarely favor coeducational schools. Despite the above conclusion, the research found that in a separate analysis of just the best studies (well-controlled) conducted in the United States, the unweighted ES in mathematics was .14 for both boys and girls. The verbal performance was .22 for girls and .13 for boys.[1] These math and verbal outcomes favoring single-sex schools parallel the findings shown above and discussed for Lee and Bryk (1989) and Mael and colleagues (2005).

The authors include studies of single-sex classrooms with studies of single-sex schools, and they control for this distinction in the analysis by treating it as a "dosage." This is a questionable strategy on two grounds. First, the advantage of single-sex schools is that these schools establish a pro-academic culture (see Chapters 7 and 8) that mitigates the youth nonacademic culture that pervade coeducational schools. It has little or nothing to do with biological/physiological differences between males and females, and it cannot be established with a set of single-sex classrooms in an otherwise coeducational school. That is, these single-sex classrooms do not provide some small single-sex school dose.

The other problem with classroom studies is that they are all different situations with varying amounts of single-sex instruction and teaching methods and context. In some, students received single-sex instruction for one hour, three times per week, in others it was every day, or for two hours, and so on. But the authors do include these classroom studies (without proper control for the amount of single-sex schooling in each classroom study) and determine that the effects for classrooms is greater than the effects for school in some cases.

Contrary to my own point of view, the effects are actually greater in classrooms than in schools. Now, obviously, I don't happen to like these results because my argument is that single-sex classrooms operate within a nonacademic culture of the coeducational school environment. And I still think it is the larger single-sex school social context that provides the pro-academic climate that defeats the anti-academic culture that pervades coeducational schools. But, maybe the classroom culture, ephemeral as it may be, is sufficient to do this, on average.

But, the most important point is that the results of this meta-analysis, once again, demonstrate the persistence of small but favorable effects for single-sex schools (and even classrooms). This is not the conclusion reached by Pahkle and colleagues, but to their credit, they provide all the evidence, and the difference between my interpretation and theirs pivots on the substantive importance of an ES. These authors seem to agree that we need more research and we need this on public schools, and this means that we need to remove the persistent obstacles to opening up more single-sex public schools in the United States.

The systematic review (Mael et al., 2005) and the recent meta-analysis (Pahlke et al., 2014) are the strongest efforts to provide a summary of the average effects on single-sex schools. Each of these analyses takes a different strategy, and each strategy has strengths and weaknesses. Mael and colleagues provide a "vote-counting" methodology, sorting studies that are statistically significant to either pro–single-sex, pro-coeducation, null, or mixed results. The advantage is that we can see the percent of studies that fall into each category. Thus, Figure 4.2 shows that there are few studies favoring coeducation, most studies are either null or favor single-sex schools, and a few studies display mixed results. The disadvantage of this approach is that they did not obtain the average results in terms of ESs.

The meta-analysis (Pahlke et al., 2014) provides these average effects, but it does not tell us what percent favor coeducational schools (very few), are mixed, are null, or favor single-sex schools. Taken together, both studies give us a picture of small favorable results for single-sex schools, but this is not the conclusion reached by Pahlke and colleagues.

Assuming that most of the null effects are about .05 and the favorable single-sex effects are about .25, the average will be about .13 (see Fig. 4.1, again). This is pretty close to the unweighted ESs for math and verbal performance shown by Pahlke and colleagues for studies done with schools in the United States (Pahlke et al., 2014: Table 6). Only these two areas have enough studies to warrant a summary conclusion in their Table 6.

I believe that both of these studies are useful, but that the average effects from Pahlke et al., 2014 can and do tilt the results against single-sex schools, especially when they employ a threshold of .2 to interpret even small results. Recall that I argue that .10 or .15 should be employed and that Mael and colleagues (2005) demonstrated that about 40 percent of the results are null and 40 percent favor single-sex schools among the forty best studies (see Fig. 4.2).

Finally, it is important to note that neither Mael and colleagues (2005) or Pahlke and colleagues (2014) give us the effects of single-sex schools in the public sector, where there are now more than 100 schools. The fact is that there are no systematic studies of these schools available. Considering these results among nonpublic schools in the United States, more research is clearly warranted on this newly emergent population of single-sex public schools. In the next chapter, I will argue and show that the effects of single-sex schools are greater for at-risk, disadvantage, urban, African American, and Latino American students and that this is true both empirically and theoretically.

NOTE

1. Pahlke et al. (2014) employed both weighted and unweighted estimates in their paper. They do this because some studies employed very large samples and weighted estimates would bias the results by exerting disproportionate influence on ESs. Nonetheless, the authors seem to rely mostly on the weighted results. For example, with reference to their Table 6 noted above, they discuss only the weighted outcomes (for the controlled studies) that are considerably smaller than the unweighted estimates that I have noted. In fairness, they make no judgment in the paper as to the preferred mode that should be used, but the weighted estimates are almost always lower.

5

+

The Effects of Single-Sex Schools Are Larger for At-Risk Students

The academic and developmental consequences of attending single-sex versus coeducational schools are significantly larger and favorable for students who are historically or traditionally disadvantaged—minorities, low- and working-class youth, or at-risk students (Bryk et al., 1993; Malcova, 2007; Riordan 1990, 1994a; Salomone, 2003; Sax, 2009). This also applies to girls or boys, depending on subject matter and on the state of the gender gap at any time. In the United States, females were on the unfavorable side of the gender gap (since the very beginning of time) until about 1985, but now males are behind females in virtually every educational indicator (DiPrete and Buchmann, 2013; Freeman, 2004; Riordan, 2003).

As a simple example of this trend in the Unites States, we can examine the bachelor's degrees awarded by sex since 1869 (Fig. 5.1). Males dominated this educational outcome until the 1980s, but by the 1990s, females are more likely to graduate from college. Efforts by those who would prefer to deny that there is a boy crisis in schools are just not credible (AAUW, 2008; Mead, 2006). The results for educational attainment are the bottom-line indicator of what has been happening for the past 150 years, as shown in Figure 5.1. Currently, the nearly 20–percentage-point difference favoring females in college graduation is predicted to increase even further by 2016, according to projections by the National Center for Educational Statistics (USED, 2012).

A similar transformation is now abundantly clear in mathematics performance, once a male-dominated subject field. Hyde and her colleagues (2008) have demonstrated that gender parity now prevails for math achievement in every grade in U.S. public schools. This is true also in the

2009 PISA study, where scores in science and mathematics for girls and boys were nearly equal in every country. And the 2009 PISA data shows that females score significantly higher on reading in every OECD country (OECD, 2009).

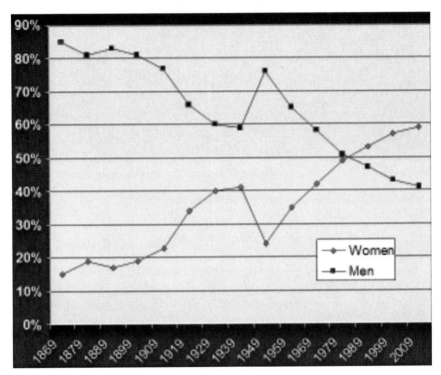

Figure 5.1.   Men Earn Fewer Degrees Than Women

Thus, the effects shown in Chapter 4 for the Lee and Bryk (1989) study and the Pahlke and colleagues (2014) meta-analysis with an average effect of .13 for studies done in the United States would be higher among at-risk students. I examined the same data (High School & Beyond) as Lee and Bryk and reported these larger effects for African American and Latino American students (Riordan, 1994a). Generally, the effect sizes favoring single-sex schools were .2 or above (Fig. 5.2).

In this study, I combined the math and reading test scores, formed a measure of leadership in curricula and extracurricular activities, and employed a measure of environmental control (locus of control). Employing a full set of background control variables, predominantly low-socio-economic-status (SES) African American and Latino American students

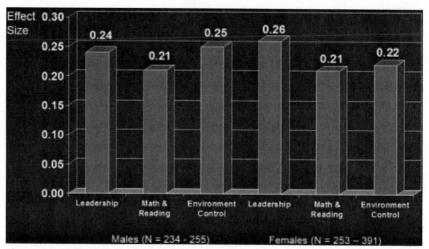

Figure 5.2. **Effect Sizes of Single Sex Schooling among African and Latino Students from Poverty Backgrounds (Riordan 1994). These are two year gain difference between students in Catholic SSS and Catholic COED schools.**

in Catholic single-sex schools outperformed their counterparts who attended Catholic coeducational schools.

High School & Beyond (HSB) sampled two types of Catholic schools. First, there was a regular Catholic school sample that generally represented all Catholic schools in the United States. In these schools, minority students constituted less than 10 percent of the student body. In addition to the regular school sample, however, HSB drew a sample of Catholic schools with a high percentage of African American and Latino students. The African American/Latino enrollment in these schools was about 50 percent in coeducational schools and 70 percent in the single-sex schools, and they were largely in urban Catholic schools.

Their test scores and SES of these students was well below the mean of the regular school sample. In short, these students were poor, at-risk, and largely African American or Latino American students. In this analysis, stringent control variables are applied for previous tests scores, SES, family structure, family size, race, school curriculum, coursework, homework, parental involvement, disciplinary climate at the school, and degree of adolescent culture present.

Some researchers have examined the concept of self-esteem as an outcome measure. There is little agreement on what factors influence self-esteem and whether a school type (single-sex or coeducational) has any significant effect. A much more important attitudinal outcome measure of success is the degree of environmental control (locus of control).

Self-esteem is an attitude that an individual takes towards oneself. Although it is surely conditioned by the environment, it is experienced by the individual as being independent of the environment. Thus, a person may feel that "I am able to do things as well as most other people," knowing full well that there are many or few obstacles to actually accomplishing certain tasks or goals. Feelings of high or low self-esteem are much like feelings that are associated with personality, such as feeling shy or extroverted.

A feeling of environmental control, however, is something quite different. Unlike self-esteem, it directly indicates the extent to which an individual feels that the social environment facilities or hinders the undertaking and completion of tasks and goals. Thus, an individual may possess high self-esteem and low environmental control. This may often be the case with at-risk children and students of color. Ross and Broh (2000) demonstrate convincingly that higher levels of locus of control are positively related to higher academic achievement, but that higher self-esteem is not related.

In my research on African American and Hispanic American students in single-sex and coeducational Catholic schools, I found that both males and females gained a significantly greater sense of environmental control over the last two years of high school, net of initial scores on the attitude measure, initial test scores, and home background (Riordan, 1994a). Moreover, this environmental control gain is entirely explained by the formal and informal single-sex school advantages, namely, higher track placement, more homework, greater parental interest, more same-sex role models, and greater discipline. This may be the most important effect of single-sex schools for disadvantaged students. *Notwithstanding other gains or losses that may result, single-sex schools provide an atmosphere that "empowers" poor, at-risk students.*

Recently, Linda Sax (2009) found that the favorable effects of single-sex schools for females was far greater in private Catholic schools than in private independent (elite) schools in the United States. Significant positive effects of Catholic single-sex schools are clearly more frequent than for independent single-sex schools. Students who attended Catholic schools (both single-sex and coed) were significantly and substantially less affluent than students attending private independent schools (both single-sex and coed). This is shown in Figure 5.3. A far greater percentage of students in private girls' independent schools than in Catholic girls' schools came from homes where the income was above $150,000 in 2009. This was especially true for single-sex independent schools. And following the argument set forth above, the number of statistically significant, favorable single-sex school effects is greater for students attending Catholic rather than the elite independent private schools.

In the Catholic schools, girls in the single-sex schools outperformed their peers who attended coeducational schools on seventeen of the twenty-three measures that were employed in the study (Fig. 5.4). In the elite independent schools, however, girls in single-sex schools did better on only eight of nineteen measures. Although these Catholic-school students were not severely disadvantaged, on average, there was clearly a substantial portion of students (about 30 percent) who were coming from homes with less than $60,000 of total family income.

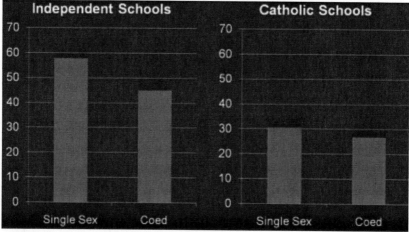

Figure 5.3.   Percent of Students Family Income Over $150,000

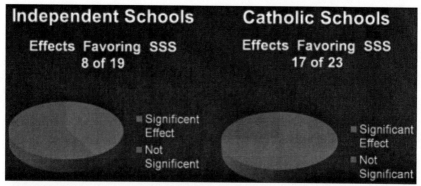

Figure 5.4.   Outcomes of Attending Single Sex or Coeducational High Schools (Achievement, Aspirations, Attitudes, and Social Behavior)

Malcova (2007) confirms this greater single-sex school effect for disadvantaged students in a recent study in England. She examined test score growth for students in the 11th grade, controlling for prior test scores in the 9th grade, along with other covariates. Students attending highly selective schools (independent and grammar) and nonselective schools (comprehensive and modern) were analyzed separately. The data were based on the entire population of students in England in 2004 with both 9th and 11th grades test scores. The results show favorable results for single-sex schools in both sectors for both boys and girls, but the single-sex school advantage is larger among lower-ability students. The major factor that conditions the strength of single-sex effects is social class, and since class and race are inextricably linked, the effects are also conditioned by race, and sometimes by gender.

Specifically, disadvantaged students in single-sex schools, compared to their counterparts in coeducational schools, have been shown to have higher achievement outcomes on standardized tests in mathematics, reading, science, and civics (Riordan, 1990). They show higher levels of leadership behavior in school, do more homework, take a stronger course load, and they also manifest higher levels of environmental control, more favorable attitudes towards school, and less sex-role stereotyping. They indicate that their schools have higher levels of discipline and order (Riordan, 1994a).

Thus, disadvantaged students (nonwhites, poor students, previously girls but now boys, and other high-risk students) stand to gain the most from single-sex schools because of the following argument: advantaged (privileged, affluent and/or high-performing) students will make their way successfully in life generally regardless of the type of school they attend, mostly because of the large effect that family resources have on educational outcomes, and for these students the effect of family resources is positive—and it is large. In effect, this context *limits* the size of the effect that a school type can actually have on these children.

Conversely, however, the effect of family resources for disadvantaged students is generally negative, and when this is joined with the negative effect of a bad school, the result is lost and doomed children. Good schools (be they small, charter, Catholic, and/or single-sex) with high-quality teachers have a greater effect on disadvantaged children because their potential influence is unlimited and unconstrained by the size and the direction of the family effect.

This is one of the most basic findings in the study of schools over the past fifty years: the effects of class size, school size, teacher quality, school resources, summer learning, the effects of oppositional culture, and reform curricula, such as Success For All, teacher expectations, and high levels of accountability in states have a greater impact on underprivileged and disadvantaged students. This basic social science finding has been shown to be true since first identified in the Coleman Report (Coleman et al., 1966; see, esp., Tables 3.221.1 and 3.221.2 on page 229). Over the past four decades, the data persistently and consistently confirm this educational fact (see Riordan, 2004).

The results for students attending women's colleges parallel and substantiate the secondary school results. These women manifest higher levels of environmental control, greater satisfaction with school (though not social life), and they achieve higher occupational success, despite the fact that there is no difference in educational achievement when compared to women who attended a coeducational college (Miller-Bernal, 2000; Riordan, 1990, 1994b).

Amazingly, women who attend a women's college for even a single year, and then transfer to a coeducational college, obtain a significant gain in occupational success (Riordan, 1994b). In this study, it was possible to separate out women who had attended a women's college for a single year, two years, three years, and so on. *The results show that attendance for just a single year is enough to increase the occupational attainment of these women. This single-sex school effect, of course, is greater for those who attend the single-sex school for longer. This is perhaps the only existing study that looks at the impact of single-sex schooling with a measurement for the number of years of actual attendance.* Most studies are for a single year only or for two years, as noted earlier in the book.

Underlying much of what I have said above is that the key measures of success in school are academic achievement and equity. Given that achievement and equality have long been recognized as the twin goals of schooling in democratic societies, we know that cognitive achievement, however it is measured, is the defining outcome of school, and that equity is obtained by comparing the achievement levels of females and males, blacks and whites, low, middle, and high SES. Reductions in the achievement gaps separating these subgroups is the best sign of equity in schools.

Despite this array of positive effects, it is important to repeat that it is not uncommon to find null or mixed results. The mixed results show that often the favorable effects are for females but not for males, or for at-risk students but not for middle-class students. Furthermore, these significant school effects are small in comparison with the much larger effects of SES and the type of curriculum in a given school. Nonetheless, the tendency favoring single-sex schooling is unmistakable.

It is important also to emphasize that white middle-class (or affluent) boys and girls do not suffer any loss by attending a single-sex school. They are not better off in coeducational schools, as shown in Figures 4.1 and 4.2 and related discussion. Moreover, there is the possibility that they do acquire small gains that are undetectable. This is consistent with the large number of null effects noted above.

6

✝

What Do We Know about Public Single-Sex Schools?

In 2003, the U.S. Department of Education contracted with RMC Research Corporation to conduct a study of existing public single-sex schools. One component of this study was the systemic review of literature that I described in Chapter 4. In addition to the systematic review, we also carried out a survey of public single-sex schools, and we did a preliminary exploratory observational study of a subsample of currently operating public single-sex schools. Both the survey and the observations were confined to those single-sex schools that were operational as of the fall of 2003.

SURVEYS AND ETHNOGRAPHIC OBSERVATIONS IN THE USED STUDY[1]

Survey and observation data provided information on the characteristics of public single-sex schooling in the United States. The study team distributed surveys in February 2005 to principals and teachers in nineteen of the twenty public single-sex schools in operation in the fall of 2003.[2] The recipients included four elementary schools, five middle schools, four middle/high schools, and six high schools. In seventeen of these schools, the students were predominantly nonwhite, and in eighteen of the nineteen schools, most students were eligible for free or reduced-price meals. Only six of the schools were in operation prior to 2000.

To draw comparisons between these public single-sex schools and coed schools, the study team analyzed the Schools and Staffing Survey (SASS) data from 150 demographically similar coed schools (the sample included

146 principals and 723 teachers). The study team used a propensity-score analysis to derive a subsample of the nationally representative SASS sample that best matched the nineteen single-sex schools on several demographic characteristics. The schools were matched on the following characteristics: the percentage of students who were African American, who were Hispanic, who were eligible for free or reduced-price meals, and the school location (i.e., urban area of a large or midsize city). The single-sex schools and the comparison schools were similar on these demographic characteristics. The study team selected 50 schools at each level (elementary, middle, and high school) for a total of 150 schools, 146 principals, and 723 teachers.

To gather more qualitative information to describe the characteristics of single-sex public schools, observation teams visited eight single-sex and two coed schools. The study team attempted to recruit two single-sex schools and two matching coed schools at each level (elementary, middle, and high school) for site-visit observations. Principals of the single-sex schools suggested coed schools in their districts that were most similar to their own schools in terms of student race and poverty level.

However, most of the coed comparison schools we contacted did not agree to participate. Because of the difficulty in obtaining cooperation from comparison schools, the sample contains only two coed comparison schools (1 elementary and 1 middle school). And because of the small number of site-visit schools (2 comparison and 8 single-sex), the sample is not representative of single-sex or coeducational schools. However, this sample does include 40 percent of the single-sex schools that were in existence at that time.

Staff and Student Characteristics

Overall, single-sex and coed school principal and teacher characteristics were similar across the two groups in terms of education. However, teachers in single-sex schools were less likely to be African American and had fewer years of teaching experience than teachers in the coed schools. Teachers in single-sex schools were also less likely to have standard certification and more likely to have probationary, temporary, or emergency certification. Student characteristics were also similar across the two samples. The majority of students in both single-sex and coed schools were African American. Note that the schools were matched, so this was to be expected.

School Programs

The single-sex schools were more likely than the coed schools to receive Title I funds, but the coed schools were more likely to offer programs for students of limited English proficiency. The single-sex schools offered more extended-day and parent-involvement programs than the coed schools, but the coed schools were more likely to have drug and violence-prevention programs. This latter finding on violence and drugs confirms the anti-academic norms likely to be present in coeducational schools.

Professional Development

The study found few differences in the percentage of teachers and principals who participated in various types of professional development. However, fewer than half of the surveyed single-sex school teachers received any professional development on single-sex education (33 percent at the elementary school level, 24 percent at the middle school level, and 15 percent at the high school level). Professional development on single-sex education was typically limited to a speaker visiting the school or a book presented to the teachers, but in a few cases single-sex education was discussed on a monthly basis. However, the professional development of teachers and principals in single-sex schools may have increased substantially since 2004 because of yearly conferences held by the national single-sex schools associations, which I noted in Chapter 1.

Perceived Benefits of Single-Sex Schooling

Principals and teachers perceived that the main benefits of single-sex schooling were decreased distractions to learning, improved student achievement, and the opportunity to address the unique learning styles and interests of boys and girls.[3] The study team collected data on the perceived advantages of single-sex schooling through the principal and teacher surveys and the site visits. The study team developed items for the principal and teacher surveys using the theoretical benefits of single-sex education that emerged from the literature review.

Table 6.1 illustrates the order of importance respondents placed on these benefits. We provided fourteen possible theoretical benefits, but Table 6.1 shows the results only for the top six chosen by the principals and teachers. Clearly, decreased distractions to learning are perceived by teachers as the primary theoretical reason for single-sex schools in the public sector.

Table 6.1. Perceived Benefits of Single-Sex Schooling

Benefit	Percent of Teachers		Percent of Principals	
	Most Important	*Included in Top 5*	*Most Important*	*Included in Top 5*
Single-sex schooling . . .				
Decreases distractions to learning.	32	72	29	76
Improves student achievement.	15	53	41	82
Addresses the unique learning styles and interests of boys or girls.	14	55	6	59
Improves student self-esteem.	7	49	0	41
Decreases the academic problems of low-achieving students.	6	24	0	35
Reduces student behavior problems.	4	40	0	47

Source: USED, 2008

Other key findings that emerged from the observational study were the following:

- The site-visit observers in the eight single-sex school sites found little evidence of substantive modifications to curricula to address the specific needs of either boys or girls, but some teachers who were interviewed provided examples of using support materials specific to the interests of girls.
- In the eight elementary and middle schools visited, site visitors observed more positive academic and behavioral interactions between teachers and students in the single-sex schools than in the comparison coed schools.
- Teachers in single-sex high schools rated problems with student behavior as less serious than teachers in coed schools, but the opposite was true in middle schools. There were no statistically significant differences between single-sex and coed school teachers' ratings of problems at the elementary school level.
- In the observational study schools, the site visitors observed more positive student interactions for the single-sex schools than for the coed comparison schools. Compared to students in the coeduca-

tional schools, students in elementary and middle single-sex schools exhibited a greater sense of community, interacted more positively with one another, showed greater respect for their teachers, were less likely to initiate class disruptions, and demonstrated more positive student role-modeling than students in the coed comparison schools. (The site visits did not include a coeducational comparison high school.)

In addition to these preliminary results from the very few public single-sex schools operating in 2005, we also know that many of the now existing 100 schools have been remarkably successful in placing their high school graduates into four-year colleges. Below, I provide the websites for those schools that I personally have visited and studied or those that are simply well-known by now. These sites speak for themselves.

http://www.brighterchoice.org/
http://www.ywln.org/who-we-are
http://www.ywln.org/all-girls-school
http://www.urbanprep.org/about
http://www.eagleharlem.org/

NOTES

1. In this section, I quote extensively from our report; see USED, 2008.
2. There were 97 single-sex schools open as of the fall of 2008, and more than 100 schools by 2014.
3. The Title IX regulations prohibit recipients from offering single-sex classes or extracurricular activities that are based on the overbroad generalizations of the different talents, capacities, or preferences of either sex.

7

+

Why Are Single-Sex Schools More Effective Than Coeducational Schools?

There are at least ten theoretical rationales that provide support for the contention that single-sex schools are more effective academically and developmentally than mixed-sex schools, especially for poor, powerless, and at-risk students. Each of these rationales is less applicable when the schools and the students are mostly from high-socioeconomic home backgrounds. These rationales are depicted in Figure 7.1.

Single-sex schools provide more successful same-sex teacher and student role models, more leadership opportunities, greater order and discipline, fewer social distractions to academic matters, and the choice of a single-sex school is a pro-academic choice (for an elaboration of these rationales, see Riordan, 1990, 1994a). Students (both males and females) also gain advantages because of significant reductions in gender bias in both teaching and peer interaction, and via access to the entire curriculum.

There is a reduction in the strength of anti-academic youth subcultures and a virtual elimination of sexual harassment and predatory behavior. And there is greater teacher sensitivity to sex differences in learning. The RMC survey of 478 teachers in public single-sex schools in the United States revealed that a *decreased distraction to learning* was the most important advantage of single-sex school by far (USED, 2008; see Fig. 6.1. I provide more detail for each of these rationales below.

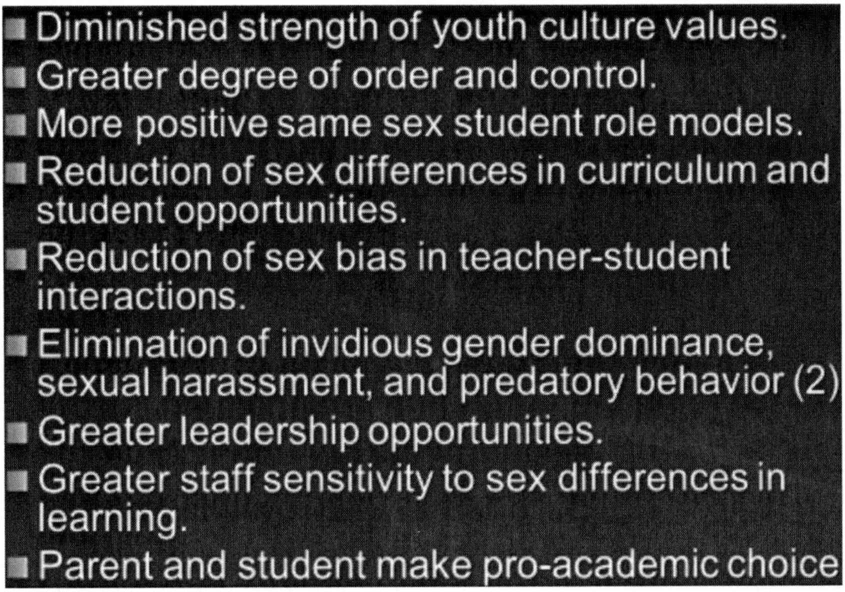

- Diminished strength of youth culture values.
- Greater degree of order and control.
- More positive same sex student role models.
- Reduction of sex differences in curriculum and student opportunities.
- Reduction of sex bias in teacher-student interactions.
- Elimination of invidious gender dominance, sexual harassment, and predatory behavior (2)
- Greater leadership opportunities.
- Greater staff sensitivity to sex differences in learning.
- Parent and student make pro-academic choice

Figure 7.1. Theoretical Rationales

1. Greater Order and Control; 2. Diminished Strength of Youth Culture Values

"Youth cultures" serve as obstacles to the existence of an "academic culture" in schools. The adolescent subculture centers on youth values—athletics, social life, physical attractiveness, popularity, soap operas, rock concerts, social media, and negative attitudes towards academic activities. Oppositional youth cultures vary from the worst possible scenarios, from drugs, violence, bullying, and crime to a less threatening, softer style. One way in which this is manifested is in the level of disciplinary problems in schools.

In schools where students frequently cut class, disobey, or talk back to teachers, it is reasonable to assume that a strong youth culture is present. Likewise, in schools where student values emphasize athletics, social life, and social media over that of academics, a strong oppositional youth culture exists. Students in schools that are characterized by a high adolescent subculture do less homework, watch more television, and score lower on cognitive tests than their counterparts attending schools with a less intense youth culture. These two rationales are inextricably linked.

Negative youth cultures are clearly more prevalent in inner city schools that are attended mostly by disadvantaged and high risk students. Black and Hispanic youth in particular are subject to the most intense forms of anti-academic culture. In predominantly Black and Hispanic schools across the country, students who aspire to succeed academically are harassed by their peers and they come to experience the "fear of acting white" (Ogbu, 2003). Oppositional youth cultures are not simply a case of greater heterosexual nonacademic interaction. Rather, they are primarily non-academic subcultures which are simply more prevalent in coeducational schools. They do exist in single-sex schools, of course, but they are easier to manage and are less dominant.

3. The Provision of More Successful Same-Sex Role Models

A second case for single-sex schooling is that it provides boys and girls a greater number of successful role models of their own sex. Teachers, counselors, and classmates model sex-appropriate behavior for all students from the earliest school years. In terms of academic outcomes, single-sex schools may be particularly advantageous for all females and minority males since the top students in *all* subjects and *all* extracurricular activities will be of their own gender and, hence, capable of serving as successful role models. This is less likely to occur in the presence of white males. In addition, the teachers in single-sex schools will be predominantly the same sex as the students.

Role models may be particularly essential for African American males. It is well documented that African American boys "turn off" from school and/or "act out" in school much earlier and to a far greater degree than white males or African American females (see Comer, 1980; Hare, 1985; Kunjufu, 1991; Steele, 1992): "The people with whom black boys . . . must interact in school do as much as (if not more than) the materials (e.g. books, etc.) and social processes (viz., the rules and regulations) to turn them off and tune them out of school" (Smith and Moore, 1992: 6).

4. The Provision of a Greater Number of Leadership Opportunities

Leadership positions in a school must be filled, regardless of talent or motivation. Every school, however effective or ineffective it may be, provides the opportunities to become involved in a wide range of regular school and extracurricular activities. Even an ineffective school will have subject matter clubs, honorary academic clubs, student council, and others. Mere participation in such clubs is a leadership opportunity, and each club provides additional opportunities in the form of elected officers.

If the student body is all-male or all-female, one can be certain that a greater number of males or females will fill these positions than they would in coeducational schools. Even if a school were entirely free of gender bias, typically there would be fewer leadership positions available for either sex. Consider a school of 1,000 students with 200 leadership slots. In a single-gender school, this means 200 opportunities for either females or males, but in a coeducational school, this means 100 opportunities for each gender. Regarding leadership opportunities, therefore, the advantages of single-sex schools are provided ipso facto. It may help if a school has favorable policies, but it may not be crucial.

5. Single-gender Schools Require a ProAcademic Parent/Student Choice

Single-sex schools are characterized by a set of values generally *shared* by parents, students, and teachers. These values stress the importance of education. A choice of single-sex education is a proacademic choice. This choicemaking process clearly involves the concept of a shared "value community," which, Coleman and Hoffer (1987) argue, makes possible the kinds of school policy decisions characteristic of effective schools. Generally, coeducation is a proadolescent subculture choice. Of course, it is typically done via school assignment.

All of the above rationales (1–5) will operate regardless of gender structure of coeducational schools. That is, even if coeducational schools were free of gender bias and gender stratification, these rationales would hold. Given the widely documented fact that coeducational schools are characterized currently by invidious forms of gender bias, sex-role stereotyping, and bullying, the following rationales (6–10) would also hold. These rationales would apply only insofar as gender stratification continues to persist in schools.

6. Sex Differences in Curricular and Extracurricular Opportunities

A sixth case for single-sex schooling is that it provides students access to the full range of the educational curricula. Historically, schools have provided different amounts and types of curricula for male and female students. In general, boys and girls have pursued different patterns of coursework, even when the actual number of years of schooling is the same. Throughout the world, boys are channeled into mathematics and science more actively, while girls are directed towards courses in languages and the humanities.

In predominantly African American/Hispanic coeducational schools in the United States, it is conceivable that this covert channeling process occurs in reverse; that is, that minority males are directed away from a more demanding academic curriculum. Single-sex schools are better able to avoid this covert channeling process.

7. A Reduction of Sex Bias in Teacher–Student Interaction

Many studies indicate that teacher–student interaction in the classroom differs systematically by sex. The salience of this problem was pointed out with the release of the report *How Schools Shortchange Women* commissioned by the American Association of University Women Educational Foundation (AAUW, 1992). This study examined more than 1,000 publications about girls and education and concluded that bias against females remained widespread in schools, and it was the cause of lasting damage to both educational achievement and self-development. These schools are coeducational schools. Quite possibly, the reverse may hold among African American/Hispanic students in the Unites States, that is, the work and the worth of males may be devalued.

8. Reduction of Sex Stereotypes; and 9. Sexual Harassment in Peer Interaction

Student peer interaction occurs throughout the school day, both in and out of the classroom. Generally, crosssex peer interaction in schools involves male dominance, male leadership, sex stereotypes, a lack of cooperation, and it often includes sexual harassment. Once again, among African American/Hispanic students, this pattern may be reversed with regard to academic matters. One can reasonably assume that the aforementioned problems are reduced in single-sex schools.

Note here that I am referring specifically to peer behavioral interaction rather than attitudes measured by a paper-and-pencil survey. Findings regarding sex stereotyping (attitudes) in single-sex and coeducational schooling are mixed, but obviously cross-sex harassment is eliminated in single-sex schools, and dominance will be reduced.

The best work on peer interaction was conducted by Elizabeth Cohen and her colleagues at Stanford University. Research has shown that small task groups, such as the typical classroom, exhibit status hierarchies where some group members are more active, influential, and powerful than others (Berger and Zelditch, 1985). These unequal status positions occur even in groups where participants have been carefully matched according to various status characteristics, such as race, gender, age, height, educational level, and occupational attainment. This process has been termed "status generalization" (Berger et al., 1974). Status generalization is a basic component of "expectation states" theory—the idea that behavior follows from expectations associated with status positions.

If dominance and inequality emerge in groups with people who are otherwise equal in societal status, it is not surprising to learn that this occurs even more predictably when group members differ in status characteristics that are viewed as unequal. Thus, since gender and race have historically been defined as unequal, expectation states theory predicts that whites and/or males will assume high-status positions in classrooms. Of course, this hierarchy may be reversed, depending on the task and the social context. For example, females always assume dominance for reading tasks in a typical classroom on average. Lockheed (1985) conducted a meta-analysis for the results by gender.

A landmark study using expectation states theory was conducted by Cohen and her colleagues at Stanford University in 1972. In Cohen's study, and several replications, it was found that simply placing African American students and white students in what appeared to be an equal-status problem-solving situation was *insufficient* to guarantee equal-status outcomes. In fact, the studies have documented and reported relatively extreme manifestations of racism—that is, white dominance.

Moreover, in these studies extensive efforts were made to alter the interaction pattern of white dominance, but with little success, except under one condition in which the African American students were literally allocated to a dominant role vis-à-vis the white students, who were allocated a submissive role. These results led Cohen and Roper (1972) to this conclusion:

> The oft made assumption that one has only to join Blacks and Whites on an officially "equal" footing in the same building for "equal status" relations to develop is not sound. . . . Belief systems concerning race and other status characteristics are so powerful that they will likely reinforce rather than damage stereotypical beliefs. (645, 657)

In addition, students hold unequal standing in the classroom based upon previous academic performance. Students hold relatively clear expectations for each other as to academic competence at various tasks (Cohen, 1994, 2000). Furthermore, the research demonstrates that group members who assume and are accorded high status in one area of expertise, such as reading, are also expected to be more competent and influential in other nonrelated tasks, academic and nonacademic. What this means for classrooms is that some students are seen as having the best ideas in specific tasks, such as reading ability, but also in most other tasks, however irrelevant they may be to reading (Rosenholz, 1985).

The results of Cohen's analyses are clear. Only by providing some form of expectancy advantage for the lower-status group are we able to consistently obtain equal-status interaction. The same findings have been reported consistently and persistently for the status characteristics of gender, age, expert status, academic status, and peer status. This has been shown in the laboratory and in the classroom.

10. Gender Differences in Learning

Over the past decades, evidence has begun to emerge suggesting that males and females may have different learning styles (Belenky et al., 1986) and a distinct style of moral reasoning (Gilligan, 1982). The authors of *Women's Ways of Knowing* (Belenky et al., 1986) argue that females are less comfortable than males with abstract intellectual argumentation that is characteristic of schooling, and that they require a heightened degree of connectedness between their own personal lives and whatever they study in the classroom.

Critics of this theory argue that it actually traps women in the stereotypes that they have been trying to dispel, and that whatever differences may exist are the result of historical gender stratification (see Faludi, 1991; Chira, 1992). The theory forms the basis for considerable debate among feminists and educators. Given the controversy surrounding the theory, one needs to be cautious about accepting it as a central rationale for single-sex schooling. Yet, as part of the overall set of rationales, it should be included.

A note regarding male/female brain differences and single-sex schools. I have indicated in Chapter 1 that there is insufficient evidence that gender-specific instruction is appropriate in single-sex schools. I want to clarify this. Males and females differ in obvious and not so obvious ways. In an often cited paper on this issue, Lenroot and colleagues (2007) demonstrate quite convincingly that males not only have larger brain volume (larger brains) but that the peak point of development of females brains occur significantly earlier than males at every stage of brain development. This comes out of study of MRI measures of the brains of males and females, who ranged in age from three to twenty-seven.

It is an intriguing but purely descriptive study and has absolutely no implications for educational practice or policy. Specifically, the authors conclude that "differences in brain size between males and females should not be interpreted as implying any sort of functional advantage or disadvantage" (1027). Despite this very specific caution, this sexual dimorphism of brain development has been cited as a basis for single-sex schooling, along with other inappropriate references. The fact is that there is no connection between brain size and attending a single-sex school and better academic or socioemotional outcomes.

Possibly by the twenty-second century, brain research will be developed to a point where the implications for education practice (and for all other aspects of our lives) will be well established, both empirically and theoretically. Currently, however, brain research is either limited to non-human animals and/or to pure laboratory studies, as noted by Lenroot and colleagues (2007). The required research is simply decades away. It is a mistake for single-sex–school advocates and practitioners to employ gender brain differences as a theoretical basis for establishing single-sex schools. It is scientifically incorrect and politically unwise.

Consider that males and females differ according to gross- and fine-motor-skill development at the beginning of kindergarten. It is pretty obvious that there are male/female differences on this important variable, and fine-motor skills, in particular, are necessary for learning to write and for later cognitive achievement (Duncan et al., 2007; Grissmer et al., 2010). But, one does not need an elaborate gender-specific pedagogy to teach boys or girls how to write. Of course, it might make sense to ask boys to write about things that they like and likewise for girls, but this could easily be accomplished in coeducational schools.

The best approach is not to emphasize gender-specific modes of instruction. Rather than this, the key, I believe, is to separate males and females in single-sex schools, thereby reducing distractions and providing all of the other advantages noted above, and to offer additional educational features, such as high-quality teachers, small classes, greater parental involvement both at school and at home, a longer school day, a longer school year, along with ongoing, objective, and sustained evaluation.

SOCIAL CAPITAL AND SINGLE-SEX SCHOOLS

The theoretical rationales and the empirical results suggest that the concept of social capital may be a fruitful way of conceiving and evaluating the value of single-sex schools for many students, but perhaps best for minorities and otherwise at-risk students. One of the most important developments in the economics of education has been that the economic concept of physical capital can be usefully and easily extended to include human capital (Schultz, 1961; Becker, 1964; Mincer, 1974). Physical capital includes land, tools, machines, and other productive equipment. The possession of physical capital facilitates the production of goods and services.

Initially, physical capital is created by working with materials to produce tools, machines, and fertile land. Likewise, human capital is generated by educating and training people to provide them with skills to increase their productivity. Hence, human capital is the possession of knowledge and skills. Schools are the main social institutions for creating and maintaining human capital. Physical capital and human capital are alike in that decision making is based largely on the expected rate of return from capital investments.

A concept closely related to human capital is *cultural capital*—the cultural resources possessed by individuals with varying degrees of human and physical capital (Bourdieu, 1987). Coleman and Hoffer (1987) argue that the idea of human capital can be extended further by incorporating the concept of social capital.

Social capital is the capacity of social institutions (such as the family, the church, or the school) to "invest" a wealth of attention, advice, support, interest, values, comfort, and care in children or students. A precondition is a minimum degree of adult or mentor presence, but the investment process is grounded in *caring relationships*. Normally, this investment involves intergenerational communication, a minimum amount of time, and selfless effort, exemplified by reading to children, helping with homework, encouraging and guiding student projects, listening to their problems, applauding their successes and comforting their failures, building self-control and social skills, and teaching basic values.

Unlike physical and human capital, where personal investment leads to an increased productivity of the self (in terms of educational and occupational achievement, fame, and fortune), social capital is an investment in the productivity of others. Social capital is a parental or institutional outlay (investment) utilized as an input by children and students towards the production of their own physical, human, and social capital. Coleman (1988: S119) calls this the *public good aspect* of social capital: "the actor or actors who generate social capital ordinarily captures only a small part of its benefits, a fact that leads to underinvestment in social capital."

How does all of this apply to single-sex schools for at-risk children? Schools, just like families, must provide some degree of social capital to help in the production of human capital. In fact, research (see Porter, 1989; Tinto, 1987; Coleman and Hoffer, 1987) clearly shows that three factors consistently influence academic success in education: academic resources (human capital), financial resources (physical capital), and social resources (social capital). Student academic success is a function of previous academic achievement and the academic quality of the school, and the amount of financial resources that they receive either from the home, the school, or both.

But schools must also provide order, discipline, encouragement, attention, security, comfort, care, trust, and identity. With regard to issues involving sex or race, schools must provide an environment that is unbiased. Certainly, to whatever extent gender bias (in either direction) exists in a school, the provision of social capital available is diminished. Given the recalcitrant track record of coeducational and predominantly white institutions, therefore, the trust, care, and attention dimensions of social capital for minority males and females may be more plentiful at single-sex schools. Social capital in schools is indicated by a high degree of interconnectedness between students, parents, and teachers.

This idea of social capital resonates with the thoughts of Larry Cuban (1991: 36), who says that single-sex schools are "desperate remedies for desperate times":

> To advocate a single-sex school . . . is, indeed, a strong response to a desperate situation. It is a turning inwards to the community, an effort to help one another because, God knows, many would say, everyone else has turned their backs. Is a desperate remedy necessarily a blemished one? What is

worthwhile about such proposals? First, they come directly from the African American community in an anguished expression of collective caring for its young. . . . In many inner cities there are too few adults on streets and in homes to offer examples of self-discipline, caring for one another, and leading a decent, lawabiding life. . . . A second point that favors the proposal is that for decades, program after program has been tried and nothing has worked to save Black boys from prison or early death. Perhaps an extreme proposal authored by African Americans for their children can do better; it certainly can't do any worse.

Clearly, proposals for single-sex schools are primarily concerned with providing social capital to children who otherwise will lose out (see also, Mitchell and Stewart, 2013).

Single-sex schools may offer an environment that is more conducive to learning than mixed-sex schools, especially for minorities. They provide more role models for students and they offer more order and control than mixed-sex schools. Women's colleges and secondary schools for girls exhibit a *low* level of typical macho and anti-academic values, allowing an academic climate to flourish. Males and females in coeducational schools are likely to experience some sex bias from teachers, counselors, or fellow students. Sex bias in single-sex schools is minimal. Mixed-sex schools do provide equality of educational opportunity, de jure. Unfortunately, the law is limited and difficult to monitor.

Beyond questions of admission, single-sex schools obviously do not discriminate by sex in providing educational opportunity. Finally, single-sex schools are characterized by a set of values generally *shared* by parents, students, and teachers. These values stress the importance of education. A choice of single-sex education is a pro-academic choice. A choice of mixed-sex education is a pro-adolescent subculture choice. This choicemaking process clearly involves the concept of a shared "value community" and the provision of "social capital," which, Coleman and Hoffer (1987) argue, makes possible the kinds of school policy decisions characteristic of effective schools.

8

+

Groups and Organizations Matter

The challenge of effective and equitable schooling in the twenty-first century is to overcome the resistance and the recalcitrance of oppositional youth cultures in and out of the school (Goodlad, 1984; Steinberg et al., 1996; Devine, 1996; Willis, 1981). This is not a new problem, and it undoubtedly predates the modern school. But, the intensity and the complexity of the problem are new, and it is the most important obstacle in the schools today. It is not just about youthful anti-intellectualism; it is not just about antisocial behavior; it is not just about athletics and rock concerts and social media; it is not just about sexual harassment; it is not just about sexual attraction and subsequent distractions; it is not just about the contentiousness that comes from increased diversity in the schools; it is about all these things and more.

Over the course of time, I have come to see the pro-academic choice that is made by parents and students as the key explanatory variable. This choice sets into motion a set of relationships among teachers, parents, and students that emphasize academics and deemphasize youth culture values, which, as I have suggested, dominate coeducational schools. I want to be absolutely clear about this point. It is not at all about sex and romance, nor is it about exclusion. It is about the rejection of anti-academic values, which predominate in our culture and our schools. Moreover, this rejection comes from the bottom up rather than the top down. In my view, it drives all that follows.

Single-sex schools, of course, provide a set of structural norms conducive to academic learning, as I outlined in Chapter 7 (see also, Riordan, 2002). This pro-academic, single-sex school social environment operates in concert and harmony with the choice-making process used by students who attend single-sex schools. In this regard, it is entirely different from a set of structures or programs that are put into place by educators.

In single-sex schools, the academic environment is normative in a true sociological sense. This idea is similar to that proposed by Bryk and colleagues (1993) of a "voluntary community" for public school policy, which would resemble Catholic schools in every respect except for religion. Similarly, KIPP (Knowledge Is Power Program) have attacked this problem successfully in coeducational schools (Angrist et al., 2012). Single-sex schools are characterized by a reciprocal relationship between organizational structures and student affirmations of those structures.

Moreover, as I have indicated, these academic definitions of school contradict the nonacademic definitions that students will otherwise bring to school and that come to constitute a youth culture. In effect, single-sex schools mitigate the single largest obstacle, which stands in the way of effective and equitable schooling, and it does this by using a fundamental sociological principle of how real social structures are created. Structures that are imposed and that contradict deeply cherished beliefs (regardless of how wrongheaded and problematic they may be) will be rejected out of hand by any group with substantial power in numbers, such as students in schools.

Single-sex schools are places where students go to learn; not to play, not to hassle teachers and other students, and not primarily to celebrate oppositional youth culture values. Aside from affluent, middle-class communities, and private and alternative schools, coeducational schools are not all about academics. This has been noted often with alarm by respected and distinguished investigators across a variety of disciplines using a variety of methodologies (Goodlad, 1984; Steinberg et al., 1996; Powell et al., 1985; Sedlack et al., 1986; Devine, 1996; Willis, 1981).

Many opponents of single-sex schools would be first in line to support the social-justice dimensions of schools. This certainly would be true on issues pertaining to race and gender gaps, sexual orientation, and inequality. But as I have indicated, the opponents are unwilling to permit single-sex schools to expand, even though they contribute, I believe, to reducing inequality and racial differences in education.

These opponents often argue that the world is gender-integrated and hence the schools must too be coeducational. But, the world is not gender-integrated among the poor and racially separated communities. Both the employed and the unemployed among the poor do not exist primarily in a coeducational worlds. This may be true for middle-class America, for students in middle-class schools, and in middle-class workplaces. But this is not true on the mean streets, in the gangs, on the ball fields, in the prisons, or in the schools of students in the inner city. Nor is it true for most middle-class athletic after school activities, such as soccer, basketball, and so on.

A recent study shows convincingly that having "lots of same-sex peers" is related to positive academic and nonacademic outcomes. Conversely, having "having lots of opposite-sex peers" is often negatively related to these same outcomes. Martin and colleagues (2009) conducted a study of 3,450 high school students ranging in age from fourteen to eighteen. They obtained student scores in both reading and mathematics and measures of student attitudes. They measured same- and opposite-sex interpersonal relationships with a set of questions, such as: "I have lots of same/opposite sex friends"; "I make friends easily with members of the same/opposite sex"; and others. The resulting correlations are shown in Figure 8.1.

Outcomes	Lots of Same Sex Peers	Lots of Opp. Sex Peers
Homework Completed	.21	.01
Enjoys School	.31	.11
Read. Score	.18	-.08
Math Score	.12	-.13

Figure 8.1. The Relative Importance of Same and Opposite Sex Peers on Academic and Non Academic Outcomes (Martin et al., 2009)

Among these students, having a greater number of same-sex friends is positively related to both reading and math scores, enjoying school, and completing homework; having a greater number of opposite-sex friends is either negatively related or not related at all to these outcomes. Since these friendships may be in or out of school, the implications of this study are that having more same-sex friends in school and/or out of school is conducive to better academic and nonacademic outcomes. It is reasonable to assume that students in single-sex schools have more same-sex friends, but this was not examined in this study.

But even in coeducational schools, Riegle-Crumb and colleagues (2006) found that girls with mostly female friends were more likely than girls with mixed-sex friends to enroll in advanced courses in high school, controlling for grades, test scores, socioeconomic status, race, and a half-dozen school and home-background variables.

Thus, I argue the most important issues are the characteristics of the groups that girls and boys belong to. And they are difficult for teachers and principals to control. But good schools are able to meet this challenge. And single-sex schools are best able to do this because the groups are separated. It is easier to provide strong discipline (control) for boys, and very little control is needed for girls in single-sex schools. *Just this small organizational change provides the advantage to single-sex schooling for both males and females.* The characteristics of boys and girls (be they innate or cultural) are of less importance than the peer groups they belong to (their associations in school, on the streets, in church, on the ball field, etc.).

It is for these reasons that I believe the best rationale for single-sex schooling is a simple one: to create groups of boys and girls that are separate for the period of time that they are in school. Within these separate groups, boys and girls should receive essentially the same curriculum. There may be some minor (and important) differences in the books used and the way that teachers teach, but these are actually less important that the single-sex grouping itself. For example, Daly and colleagues (1998) demonstrated convincingly that boys perform much better in reading when the material is enjoyable and aligned with their interests. As I noted, boys will require more control and girls less control, all made easier by the separate grouping (see Riordan, 1990).

So to summarize, the unique characteristics of the gender groups are more important than the characteristics of boys or girls as individuals. Treating these group differences is not easy because they are powerful and they do affect the learning process. I am not saying that innate and cultural gender differences are nonexistent, but only that the effect on the learning process is less than the gender-grouping effect.

Some people still think the gender gap is a one-way street, with males enjoying all the advantages. Beyond the schoolhouse door, this may still be true, but in elementary and secondary schools, this is simply not true, and perhaps never was correct. Recent reports have now confirmed that boys are on the unfavorable side of the gender gap in education and developmental matters (USED, 2000; Hedges and Nowell, 1995; Lee et al., 1995; Linn and Hyde, 1989; Nowell 1997; Riordan, 2003; Willingham and Cole, 1997). What is becoming increasingly clear is that coeducational schools will have to provide special attention to boys in reading, writing, and engagement, and this is going to complicate the entire equation for creating equity in coeducational schools.

WHAT ARE THE IMPLICATIONS FOR
SINGLE-SEX PUBLIC SCHOOLS?

Single-sex schools remain an effective form of school organization for disadvantaged students in public schools. The schools provide a structure that is conducive to learning. In selecting a single-sex school with its structure in place, students reject the anti-academic norms that permeate most public coeducational schools attended by at-risk youth. They make a pro-academic choice. I have no illusions that students do this gleefully and go off to school dancing in the streets. Of course, for most students the choice is made by parents for their children. But the point is this: *an effective school requires a minimal level of compliance (even if it is begrudging) on the part of the students to the academic norms of the school.*

Specifically, in order for a school to provide high levels of achievement and equity for students, it should provide a challenging academic program to all students, the teaching style should be active and constructive, the relationships among teachers, administrators, parents, and students should be communal, and the school should be small. Youth culture, anti-academic values should be minimized, order and control should prevail, successful student role models should be abundant, sex (and race) bias in peer interaction and student–teacher interaction should be nonexistent, and leadership and educational opportunities should be free of sex (and race) bias.

One can certainly try to set this up by instituting rules and regulations, structures and norms from the desks of superintendents, principals, and policy wonks. And in lieu of any other alternative, this is how it will be done. But institutions simply do not work very well that way, especially when the clients are youth, who understandably and justifiably want a stake in the creation of social organizations that ultimately control their behavior. Single-sex schools provide an avenue for students to make a pro-academic choice, thereby affirming their intrinsic agreement to work in the kind of environment that we identify as an effective and equitable school.

Single-sex schools should not be expected to correct all the problems that exist in society and in coeducational schools. Nor should anyone fear that their existence would detract in any way from efforts that should be made to provide greater effectiveness in public coeducational schools. Moreover, all students do not automatically do better in single-sex schools. The important thing is the selection of a type of school that best suits each individual student.

Single-sex schools in both the public and private sectors should incorporate the preconditions for single-sex teaching advocated by Younger and Warrington (2006). These include a firm embrace of the single-sex approach, a strong commitment to objective evaluation, a strong sense of collaboration among the entire school staff, commitment to identifying and refining teaching strategies that do not emphasize gender-specific pedagogy (evidence is too weak), and several other unique structural features (see Fig. 8.2).

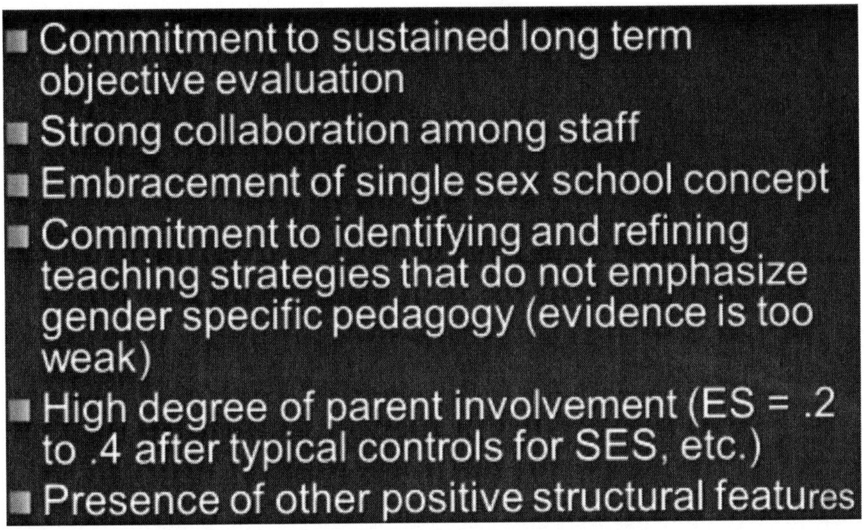

- Commitment to sustained long term objective evaluation
- Strong collaboration among staff
- Embracement of single sex school concept
- Commitment to identifying and refining teaching strategies that do not emphasize gender specific pedagogy (evidence is too weak)
- High degree of parent involvement (ES = .2 to .4 after typical controls for SES, etc.)
- Presence of other positive structural features

Figure 8.2. Conditions for Success of Single Sex Schools Younger and Warrington (2006)

In the end, I want to point out that much is simply not known about the relative effectiveness of single-sex and coeducational schooling. The bottom line is that no one in the world knows with any reasonable degree of certainty, either empirically, theoretically, or philosophically, at what educational level single-sex schools might be more effective or less effective, or in what subject, or in what personal developmental area they might be more or less effective. Largely because of political opposition, research on single-sex schools is in its infancy. The best days are ahead, I hope.

What we do know with a reasonable degree of certainty is that, in general, single-sex schools are more effective than coeducational schools, and conversely, in general, that coeducational schools are not more effective nor are they more equitable. On average, students attending a single-sex school will either do no better or no worse than comparable students in coeducational schools, or they will gain small but significant and substantial educational and socioemotional advantages. This makes single-sex schools a wise choice, especially for at-risk and disadvantaged students.

Moreover, if the schools are equally effective, on average, students should be allowed the opportunity to attend, and the parents to choose, the one they like best so long as they do so within existing law.

It may be that single-sex schools are more effective as middle schools, but not as elementary and high schools, or that they work only if you have a full dose from kindergarten through high school. It may be that single-sex schools improve math and science scores for girls and they might improve reading, writing, and engagement for boys, and this would lead to greater gender equality for each sex where there currently exists a gender gap. One or the other of these organizational forms may be better suited in some countries than in others.

Moreover, the theoretical rationales (which in science are equally important to the empirical results) for why single-sex schools would be more or less effective in which areas and at which grades and for which students are not at all clear. Without rigorous theoretical models that lead to scientific empirical studies, all sorts of unsubstantiated theoretical whims are invented and passed around and, as we all know, enter quickly into the media.

In fact, these theoretical whims (or pseudo-facts) enter into the media more quickly by far than the real scientific theories. Thus, we need to be careful about advancing theories for why single-sex schools might provide advantages for boys and/or for girls. We need to be especially careful about advancing hard-wired brain theories that have the least amount of credibility in terms of education practice. Further, we need to adopt an open stance vis-à-vis the research questions and take the high road of promoting and accepting only the highest quality of research available on the subject. To do otherwise is to be an irresponsible producer and/or consumer of educational research.

Of course, opponents of single-sex schools also urge caution, but this is usually disingenuous and politically motivated. To the opponents, I say the only way to obtain answers to these questions is by conducting research on single-sex schools, especially in the public sector, where desperate, powerless, and poor children suffer and have suffered for too long in schools that do not help them to attain the dreams that all children and their parents cherish.

Taking an oppositional stance towards single-sex public schools and at the same time taking a stance against allowing further research is an anti-scientific position. The education of our children is too important to be decided entirely on political or ideological grounds alone. And this is especially true and absolutely necessary when we consider that the children most likely to benefit from a more effective school are impoverished children.

We need to provide some basis for allowing a sufficient number of public single-sex schools to open so that at least over a reasonable period of time we can obtain answers to these questions. This is not an easy task, even without politicalizing the issue, because just doing the empirical studies involves very complex scientific educational research.

References

Alexander K. L., and A. M. Pallas. 1985. "School Sector and Cognitive Performance: When Is a Little a Little?" *Sociology of Education* 58:115–28.

Allison, P. D. 1999. *Multiple Regression*. Thousand Oaks, CA: Pine Forge.

AAUW (American Association of University Women). 1998. *Gender Gaps*. Washington, DC: American Association of University Women Educational Foundation.

———. 1992. *How Schools Shortchange Girls*. Washington, DC: American Association of University Women Educational Foundation.

———. 2008. *Where the Girls Are: The Facts about Gender Equity in Education*. Washington, DC: American Association of University Women Educational Foundation.

Angrist, J. D., S. M. Dynarski, T. J. Kane, P. A. Pathak, and C. R. Walters. 2012. "Who Benefits from KIPP?" *Journal of Policy Analysis and Management* 31(4):837–60.

Becker, G. S. 1964. *Human Capital*. Chicago: University of Chicago Press.

Belenky, M. F., B. M. Clinchy, N. R. Goldberger, and J. M. Tarule. 1986. *Women's Ways of Knowing*. New York: Basic Books.

Berger, J., T. L. Conner, and M. H. Fisek (eds.). 1974. *Expectation States Theory*. Cambridge, MA: Winthrop.

Berger, J., and M. Zelditch, Jr. (eds.). 1985. *Status, Rewards, and Influence*. San Francisco: Jossey-Bass.

Bloom, H., C. Hill, A. R. Black, and M. Lipsey. 2006. *Effect Sizes in Education Research: What They Are, What They Mean, and Why They're Important*. Washington, DC. Institute of Education Sciences Research Conference.

Borman, G., and M. Dowling. 2010. "Schools and Inequality: A Multilevel Analysis of Coleman's Equality of Educational Opportunity Data." *Teachers College Record* 112(5):1201–46.

Bourdieu, P. 1987. The Forms of Cultural Capital. In *Handbook of Theory andResearch for the Sociology of Education.* (J. G. Richardson. Ed.). Westport, CN: Greenwood Presd, 241-258

Bracey, G.W. 2006. *Separate but Superior? A Review of Issues and Data Bearing on Single-Sex Education.* College of Education Division of Educational Leadership and Policy Studies, Arizona State University, Tempe, 85287-241.1.

Bryk, A. S., V. E. Lee, and P. B. Holland. 1993. *Catholic Schools and the Common Good.* Cambridge, MA: Harvard University Press.

Bureau of Education. 1883. *Co-education of the Sexes in the Public Schools of the U.S.A.* Washington, DC: United States Government Printing Office.

Butler, N. M. (ed.). 1910. *Education in the United States.* New York: American Book Company.

Chira, S. (1992, February 12). "Bias Against Girls is Found Rife in Schools, with Lasting Damage." *New York Times.*

Cohen, E. G. 1994. *Designing Groupwork: Strategies for the Heterogeneous Classroom.* 2nd ed. New York: Teachers College Press.

————. 2000. "Equitable Classrooms in a Changing Society." In *Handbook of the Sociology of Education,* edited by M. Hallinan. New York: Kluwer.

Cohen, E. G., and S. S. Roper. 1972. "Modification of Interaction Disability: An Application of Status Characteristics Theory." *American Sociological Review* 37:643–57.

Cohen, J. 1988. *Statistical Power Analysis for the Behavioral Sciences.* Hillsdale, NJ: Erlbaum.

Coleman, J.S. 1968. The Concept of Equality of Educational Opportunity. *Harvard Educational Review.* 38: 17-22

Coleman, J. S. 1988. Social Capital in the Creation of Human Capital. *American Journal of Sociology,* 94, Supplement: Organizations and Institutions: Sociological and Economic Approaches to the Analysis of Social Structure, S95-S120, University of Chicago Press.

Coleman, J. S., E. Q. Campbell, C. J. Hobson, J. McPartland, A. M. Mood, F. Weinfeld, and R. L. York. 1966. *Equality of Educational Opportunity.* Washington, DC: U.S. Government Printing Office.

Coleman, J. S., and T. Hoffer. 1987. *Public and Private High Schools. The Impact of Communities.* New York: Basic Books.

Comer, J. P. 1980. *School Power: Implication for an Intervention Project.* New York: Free Press.

Cuban, L. 1991. "Desperate Remedies for Desperate Times." *Education Week* 11 (November 20): 36.

Daly, P., J. Salters, and C. Burns. 1998. "Gender and Task Interaction: Instant and Delayed Recall of Three Story Types." *Educational Review* 50:269–75.

Devine, J. 1996. *Maximum Security: The Culture of Violence in Inner-City Schools.* Chicago: University of Chicago Press.

DiPrete, T., and C. Buchmann. 2013. *The Rise of Women: The Growing Gender Gap in Education and What It Means for American Schools.* New York: Russell Sage Foundation.

Duncan, G. J., C. J. Dowsett, A. Claessens, K. Magnuson, A. C. Huston, P. Klebanov et al. 2007. "School Readiness and Later Achievement." *Developmental Psychology* 43:1428–46.

Ewing, E. T. 2006. "The Repudiation of Single-Sex Education: Boys' Schools in the Soviet Union, 1943–1954." *American Educational Research Journal* 43:621–50.

Faludi, S. 1991. *Backlash: The Undeclared War against the American Woman.* New York: Crown.

Foucault, M. 1968. "Foucault Répond à Sartre." *La Quinzaine Litteraire* 46:20–22.

Freeman, C. E. 2004. *Trends in Educational Equity of Girls & Women: 2004.* U.S. Department of Education, National Center for Education Statistics. Washington, DC: U.S. Government Printing Office.

Gilligan, C. 1982. *In a Different Voice: Psychological Theory and Women's Development.* Cambridge, MA: Harvard University Press.

Goodlad, J. 1984. *A Place Called School.* New York: McGraw-Hill.

Grissmer, D., K. J. Grimm, S. M. Aiyer, W. M. Murrah, and J. S. Steele. 2010. "Fine Motor Skills and Attention: Primary Developmental Predictors of Later Achievement." *Developmental Psychology* 46:1008–17.

Gurian, M., and A. Ballew. 2003. *The Boys and Girls Learn Differently Action Guide for Teachers.* New York: John Wiley.

Halpern, D. F., L. Eliot, R. S. Bigler, R. A. Fabes, L. D. Hanish, J. Hyde, L. S. Liben, and C. L. Martin. 2011. "The Pseudoscience of Single-Sex Schooling." *Science* 333: 1706–7.

Hedges, L. V., and A. Nowell. 1995. "Sex Differences in Mental Test Scores, Variability, and Numbers of High-Scoring Individuals." *Science* 269: 41–45.

Heyneman S. P. 2014. "Research Quality: Quantitative or Qualitative?" *Teachers College Record.* January 31. https://my.vanderbilt.edu/stephenheyneman/files/2011/09/TC-Record-article-January-2014.pdf.

Hoffer, T., A. M. Greeley, and J. S. Coleman, J. S. 1985. "Achievement Growth in Public and Catholic Schools." *Sociology of Education* 58:74–97.

Hyde, J. S., S. M. Lindberg, M. C. Linn, A. B. Ellis, and C. C. Williams. 2008. "Gender Similarities Characterize Math Performance." *Science* 321:494–95.

Jencks, C. 1985. "How Much Do High School Students Learn?" *Sociology of Education* 58: 128–35.

Kim, D. H., and H. Law. 2011. "Gender Gap in Maths Test Scores in South Korea and Hong Kong: Role of Family Background and Single-Sex Schooling." *International Journal of Educational Development* 32:92–103.

Klein, S., J. Lee, P. McKinsey, and C. Archer. 2014. *Identifying U.S. K-12 Public Schools with Deliberate Sex Segregation.* Arlington, VA: Feminist Majority Foundation.

Kolesnik, W. B. 1969. *Co-education: Sex Differences and the Schools.* New York: Vantage.

Kozol, J. 1991. *Savage Inequalities.* New York: Broadway.

Kunjufu, J. 1991. *Countering the Conspiracy to Destroy Black Youth.* Chicago: African American Images.

Lee, V. E., and A. S. Bryk. 1986. "Effects of Single-Sex Secondary Schools on Students Achievement and Attitudes." *Journal of Educational Psychology* 78:381–95.

———. 1989. Effects of Single-Sex Schools: Response to March. *Journal of Educational Psychology* 81(4):647–50.

Lee, V. E., X. Chen, and B. A. Smerdon. 1995. *The Influence of School Climate on Gender Differences in Achievement and Engagement of Young Adolescents.* Washington, DC: American Association of University Women.

Lenroot, R. K., N. Godtay, D. K. Greenstein, E. M. Wells, G. L. Wallace, L. S. Clasen, J. D. Blumenthal, J. Lerch, A. P. Zijdenbos, A. C. Evens, P. M. Thompson, and J. Giedd. 2007. "Sexual Dimorphism of Brain Developmental Trajectories during Childhood and Adolescence." *NeuroImage* 36:1065–73.

Linn, M. C., and J. S. Hyde. 1989. "Gender, Mathematics, and Science." *Educational Researcher* 18: 17–27.

Lockheed, M. E. 1985. "Sex and Social Influence: A Meta-Analysis Guided by Theory." In *Status, Rewards, and Influence*, edited by J. Berger and M. Zelditch, Jr., 406–27. San Francisco: Jossey-Bass.

Mael, F., A. Alonso, D. Gibson, K. Rogers, and M. Smith. 2005. *Single-Sex versus Coeducational Schooling: A Systematic Review.* Washington, DC: U.S. Department of Education.

Malcova, E. 2007. "Effect of Single-Sex Education on Progress in GSSE." *Oxford Review of Education* 33:233–59.

Martin, A. J., H. W. Marsh, D. M. McInerney, and J. Green. 2009. "Young People's Interpersonal Relationships and Academic and Nonacademic Outcomes: Scoping the Relative Salience of Teachers, Parents, Same-Sex Peers, and Opposite Sex Peers." *Teachers College Record* (March 23):1–6. http://www.tcrecord.org/Content.asp?ContentId=15593.

Marsh, H. W. 1989. "Effects of Attending Single-Sex and Coeducational High Schools on Achievement, Attitudes, Behavior, and Sex Differences." *Journal of Educational Psychology* 81(1):70–85.

———. 1991. "Public, Catholic Single-Sex, and Catholic Coeducational High Schools: Effects on Achievement, Affect, and Behaviors." *American Journal of Education* 11:320–56.

Mead, S. 2006. *The Truth about Boys and Girls.* Washington, DC: Education Sector.

Miller-Bernal, L. 2000. *Separate by Degree: Women Students' Experiences in Single and Coeducational Colleges.* New York: Peter Lang.

Mincer, J. 1974. *Schooling, Experience, and Earnings.* New York: National Bureau of Economic Research.

Mitchell, A. B., and J. B. Stewart. 2013. "The Efficacy of All-Male Academies: Insights from Critical Race Theory (CRT)." *Sex Roles* 69(7/8):382–92.

Neumann, A. 2006. "Professing Passion: Emotion in the Scholarship of Professors at Research Universities." *American Education Research Journal* 43(3):381–424.

Nowell, A. 1997. "Trends in Gender Differences in Academic Achievement from 1960 to 1994." Paper presented at the annual meeting of the American Educational Research Association.

Ogbu, J. U. 2003. *Black American Students in an Affluent Suburb: A Study of Academic Disengagement.* New York: Lawrence Erlbaum.

O'Keefe, J. M., and J. Murphy. 2000. "Ethnically Diverse Catholic Schools: School Structure, Students, Staffing, and Finance." In *Catholic Schools at the Crossroads*, edited by J. Youniss and J. J. Convey. New York: Teachers College Press.

OECD (Organisation for Economic Co-operation and Development). 2009. "Equally Prepared for Life? How 15-Year-Old Boys and Girls Perform in School." Paris. http://www.oecd.org/fr/education/scolaire/programmein-ternationalpourlesuividesacquisdeselevespisa/equallypreparedforlifehow15-year-oldboysandgirlsperforminschool.htm.

Pahlke, E., J. S. Hyde, and C. M. Allison. 2014. "The Effects of Single-Sex Compared with Coeducational Schooling on Students' Performance and Attitudes: A Meta-Analysis." *Psychological Bulletin* 140(4):1042–72.

Pahlke, E., J. S. Hyde, and J. E. Mertz. 2013. "The Effects of Single-Sex Compared with Coeducational Schooling on Mathematics and Science Achievement: Data from Korea." *Journal of Educational Psychology* 105(2):444–52.

Park, H, J. R. Behrman, and J. Choi. 2013. "Causal Effects of Single-Sex Schools on College Entrance Exams and College Attendance: Random Assignment in Seoul High Schools." *Demography* 50:447–69.

Porter, O. F. 1989. *Undergraduate Completion and Resistance at Four Year Colleges and Universities*. Washington, DC: National Institute for Independent Colleges and Universities.

Powell, A. G., E. Farrar, and D. K. Cohen. 1985. *The Shopping Mall High School: Winners and Losers in the Educational Market Place*. Boston: Houghton Mifflin.

Riegle-Crumb, C., G. Farkus, and C. Muller. 2006. "The Role of Gender and Friendship in Advanced Course Taking." *Sociology of Education* 79:206–28.

Riordan, C. 1984. "Public and Catholic Schooling: Cognitive Outcomes in Context." Paper presented at the annual meeting of the American Educational Research Association.

———. 1985. "Public and Catholic Schooling: The Effect of Gender Context Policy." *American Journal of Education* 93:518–40.

———.1990. *Girls and Boys in School: Together or Separate?* New York: Teachers College Press.

———.1994a. "Single-Gender Schools: Outcomes for African and Hispanic Americans." *Research in Sociology of Education and Socialization* 10:177–205.

———.1994b. The Value of Attending a Women's College. *Journal of Higher Education* 65(4):486–510.

———. 2000. "Trends in Student Demography in Catholic Secondary Schools, 1972–1992." In *Catholic Schools at the Crossroads*, edited by J. Youniss and J. J. Convey. New York: Teachers College Press.

———. 2002. "What Do We Know about the Effects of Single-Sex Schools in the Private Sector? Implications for Public Schools." In *Gender in Policy and Practice*, edited by A. Datnow and L. Hubbard. New York: Routledge Falmer.

———. 2003. "Failing in School? Yes; Victims of War? No." *Sociology of Education* 76:369–72.

———. 2004. *Equality and Achievement: An Introduction to the Sociology of Education*. 2nd ed. New York: Addison Wesley Longman.

Rosenholtz, S. J. 1985. "Modifying Status Expectations in the Traditional Classroom." In *Status, Rewards, and Influence*, edited by J. Berger and M. Zelditch, Jr., 445–70. San Francisco: Jossey-Bass.

Ross, C. E., and B. A. Broh. 2000. "The Roles of Self-Esteem and the Sense of Personal Control in the Academic Achievement Process." *Sociology of Education* 73:270–84.

Sadker, M., and D. Sadker. 1994. *Failing at Fairness: How America's Schools Cheat Girls.* New York: Charles Scribner's Sons.

Salomone, R. 1996. *Rich Girls, Poor Girls, and the Perils of Ideology.* Keynote Address, Annual Leadership Conference of the Connecticut Chapter of the American Association of University Women, Wesleyan University.

———. 2003. *Same, Different, Equal: Rethinking Single-Sex Schooling.* New Haven, CT: Yale University Press.

———. 2013. "Rights and Wrongs in the Debate over Single-Sex Schooling." *Boston University Law Review* 93:971–1027.

Sax, L. 2005. *Why Gender Matters: What Parents and Teachers Need to Know about the Emerging Science of Sex Differences.* New York: Random House.

Sax. L. J. 2009. *Women Graduates of Single-Sex and Coeducational High Schools: Differences in Their Characteristics and the Transition to College.* Los Angeles: The Sudikoff Family Institute for Education & New Media, UCLA Graduate School of Education & Information Studies.

Schultz, T. W. 1961. "Investment in Human Capital." *American Economic Review* 51:1–17.

Sedlak, M. W., C. W. Wheeler, D. C. Pullin, and P. A. Cusick. 1986. *Selling Students Short: Classroom Bargains and Academic Reform in the American High School.* New York: Teachers College Press.

Signorella, M. L., A. R. Hayes, and Y. Li, 2013. A Meta-Analytic Critique of Mael et al.'s (2005) Review of Single-Sex Schooling. *Sex Roles* 69:423–41.

Smith, A. W., and E. G. J. Moore. 1992. "Positive Segregation: The Consequences of Separate Schools for African-American Males." Paper presented at the annual meeting of the American Educational Research Association.

Smithers, A., and P. Robinson. 2006. *The Paradox of Single-Sex and Co-educational Schooling.* Buckingham, U.K.: Carmichael.

Steele, C. M. 1992. "Race and the Schooling of Black Americans." *The Atlantic* 269:68–78.

Steinberg, L. B., B. Brown, and S. M. Dornbusch. 1996. *Beyond the Classroom.* New York: Simon and Schuster.

Tidball, M. E., D. G. Smith, C. S. Tidball, and L. E. Wolf-Wendel. 1999. *Taking Women Seriously: Lessons and Legacies for Educating the Majority.* Phoenix: American Council on Education and Oryx Press.

Tinto, V. 1987. *Leaving College.* Chicago: University of Chicago Press.

Tyack, D., and S. L. Hansot, 1990. *Learning Together: A History of Coeducation in American Schools.* New Haven, CT: Yale University Press.

USED (U.S. Department of Education). 2000. *Trends in Educational Equity of Girls and Women.* Washington, DC. Office of Educational Research and Improvement, NCES, 2000-03.

———. 2005. National Center for Education Statistics. Washington, DC: U.S. Government Printing Office (NCES 2005-016).

———. 2006. Rules and Regulations. Federal Register: October 25, Vol. 71, No. 206, 62529-62543.

———. 2007. *The Condition of Education, 2007.* National Center for Education Statistics. Washington, DC. U.S. Government Printing Office, 2007-064.

———. 2008. Office of Planning, Evaluation and Policy Development, Policy and Program Studies Service. *Early Implementation of Public Single-Sex Schools: Perceptions and Characteristics,* Washington, DC. Contract to RMC Research Corporation, Portland, OR.

_____. 2012. Digest of Education Statistics. Washington, DC. U.S. Government Printing Office, Table 310.

———. 2014. Office of Civil Rights. *Questions and Answers on Title IX and Single-Sex Elementary and Secondary Classes and Extracurricular Activities.* http://www.whitehouse.gov/sites/default/files/omb/fedreg/2007/012507_good_guidance.pdf.

Willingham, W. W., and N. S. Cole. 1997. *Gender and Fair Assessment.* Mahwah, NJ: Lawrence Erlbaum.

Willis, P. 1981. *Learning to Labor: How Working-Class Kids Get Working-Class Jobs.* New York: Columbia University Press.

Wilson, W. J. 1987. *The Truly Disadvantaged: The Inner City, the Underclass, and Public Policy.* Chicago: University of Chicago Press.

Wiseman, A. W. 2008. "A Culture of (In)Equality? A Cross National Study of Gender Parity and Gender Segregation in National School Systems." *Research in Comparative and International Education* 3:179–201.

Younger, M. R., and M. Warrington. 2006. "Would Harry and Hermione Have Done Better in Single-Sex Classes? A Review of Single-Sex Teaching in Co-educational Secondary Schools in the United Kingdom." *American Education Research Journal* 43:559–620.